The Library of Liberal Arts

OSKAR PIEST, *General Editor*

[NUMBER SEVENTY-SEVEN]

THE EPIC OF THE CID

Cantar de mío Cid

THE EPIC OF
THE CID

Translated, with an Introduction, by
J. GERALD MARKLEY
Associate Professor of Spanish and Latin, University of Wichita

A LIBERAL ARTS PRESS BOOK

THE **BOBBS-MERRILL** COMPANY, INC.
A SUBSIDIARY OF HOWARD W. SAMS & CO., INC.
Publishers • INDIANAPOLIS • NEW YORK

861
C229cE
1961

CONTENTS

CONTENTS

INTRODUCTION

The *Poem of the Cid,* which was composed in the twelfth century, is the oldest Spanish epic in existence. Just as the Greek, French, and German epics were composed at early stages in the development of their respective literatures, this epic, written in a rough and rugged style, appeared at an early date in Spanish literary history.

The poem is based on a historical character, Rodrigo Díaz de Vivar, popularly called The Cid (from the Arab title El Seid, the lord) and El Campeador—the champion. Its action takes place in the eleventh century, when the historic Cid lived, and at a time when Christian Spain was divided into the kingdoms of León, Castile, Aragón, and Navarre. The contending kingdoms delayed the reconquest and unification of the Spanish peninsula until the reign of Ferdinand and Isabella in the latter half of the fifteenth century.

The epic unfolds against this background of struggle for power and position a vivid picture of its age. In the first canto, the Cid has become a victim of rumors spread by his rivals at court and has been ordered into exile by King Alfonso. Leaving his wife and two daughters in the care of the Abbot of the monastery of San Pedro de Cardeña, the Cid departs from Castile accompanied into exile by loyal vassals and friends. He is joined by many other knights who follow him because of his reputation as a noble warrior; as a soldier of fortune, raiding Christians and Moors alike, he wins one battle after another. The Cid attempts to regain favor with Alfonso by sharing with him his immense booty.

The adventures of the second canto culminate in the Cid's capture of the great city of Valencia from the Moors. By consent of King Alfonso, his wife Jimena and his daughters Doña Elvira and Doña Sol are reunited with him in Valencia. The women are given a chance to watch the Cid's knights "win their bread" while engaged in a defense of the city. After the victory and a reconciliation with Alfonso, the Infantes de Carrión, who covet the Cid's wealth, ask for his daughters in marriage. Reluctant to consent, he consults the King and on his advice decides to permit the wedding. The Infantes come to Valencia, where great wedding festivities are celebrated.

But in the third canto, the Infantes, now the Cid's sons-in-law, display their complete cowardice in several episodes which makes them objects of ridicule to all but the Cid. Their humiliation and shame are transformed into a violent hatred for the Cid and his daughters. By a ruse, they succeed in taking their wives on a journey to their estates in Carrión. The Infantes have many costly gifts with them as well. In accordance with their plans, they halt in the Forest of Corpes and beat the two women shamefully, and abandon them half dead. The Cid's nephew, Félix Muñoz, who has suspected some treachery, rescues the Cid's daughters and takes them back to the Cid in Valencia. The Cid seeks and gains redress through King Alfonso; all the wealth he has given the Infantes is restored to him and a judicial combat is arranged to restore his honor. In this tourney his companions defeat the Infantes de Carrión. Hearing of the dissolution of the marriages, the wealthy and honorable Infantes of Navarre and Aragón sue for and marry the Cid's daughters.

The fantastic and supernatural elements in epics such as *Beowulf,* the *Iliad,* the *Aeneid,* the *Nibelungenlied,* and *Roland* are entirely lacking in *The Cid.* The Cid in the epic retains close ties with reality insofar as realistic actions occur and realistic detail is described; he fights no dragons, suffers no enchantments, nor is he ever enveloped by clouds and borne to safety as a result of divine intervention—although when one considers the fearful odds against the Cid in battle, his victories are sometimes little short of miraculous.

The Cid as a romantic character is familiar to western literature for the most part through Corneille's play *Le Cid* (1636), an adaptation of *Mocedades del Cid,* 'Exploits of the Young Cid,' by Guillén de Castro (1569-1631). The latter was the first dramatization of the Cid legend as told in the ballads (Sp. *romances*), translated into English by Robert Southey. These ballads, first collected in the sixteenth century, are characterized, unlike the epic poem, by extravagant adventures and great liberties with historical fact.

The Cid of the epic, however, becomes the epitome of the Spanish hero. His portrayal is sober and restrained without romantic idealization. The Cid is depicted as having unwavering courage, honor, loyalty, family love, sincere religious devotion and even a certain spirit of democracy—ideals which have persisted in Spanish life and literature.

The poet has allowed himself considerable license of chronology, and the poetic Cid is not the historical man who consorted with the enemies of his king. But the events of the epic have a historical veracity unusual in such literature. Almost every character and geographical location have been authenticated.

The treatment of events gives us glimpses of medieval pageantry, the complexities of vassalage, and pictures of a warrior-bishop, soldiers exhilarated by both Moorish and Christian booty; we even hear the sound of Moorish battle drums—all these particulars create a tapestry of historical and social authenticity.

Much of this detail could be found in non-literary sources, and although we find a picture of medieval Spanish life in *The Cid,* we also find an exciting story well told. The strange characterization of events is a crystallization of the spirit of this epoch. And it is in the Cid, a character so completely expressive of the ideals of his time, that we find an epic hero of significant stature.

In keeping with the whole realistically rooted conception of this epic, the Cid never is idealized into a demi-god. It is true that the historical Cid was the greatest knight, the most successful troop commander, and one of the best political administrators of his time; beyond that we find his qualities of generosity and greatness of character artfully exhibited against the series of events of the poem.

The *Cantar de mio Cid* was composed by some unknown minstrel about the year 1140, although the date of composition may have been as much as half a century later. We can be certain, however, that the epic was composed at a time when the exploits of the Cid were still a clear and compelling memory to the people of Spain, for the Cid could have been dead no more than a century when the poem was written—a unique occurrence in epic poetry.

The Cid consists of approximately 3,800 lines, rhyming in assonance. In this translation, the manuscript sections are numbered consecutively with each change of rhyme in the poem.

The translator laments the overwhelming loss of literary values inherent in translating a work of twelfth-century Spanish poetry into modern English prose. While it has been possible to preserve the very few metaphors employed by the poet, the effects of rhyme, rhythm, word order, euphony, and other devices of poetical form are enfeebled or lost altogether. The effort has necessarily been restricted to achieving a clear, readable version which reproduces as faithfully as possible the meaning of the original work. The use of obscure archaisms and of a word order abnormal to the language of the translation accomplishes little more than the introduction of a third language into the problem of translation, and such use has been zealously avoided. It is hoped that the retention of the heroic epithets, the redundancies of expression, and of the stock phraseology will suffice to suggest the tone of the original.

J. GERALD MARKLEY

NOTE ON THE TEXT

Only one manuscript of *The Cid* is extant, a copy made by one Per Abat which bears the date 1307. This manuscript was found at Vivar and first published by Tomás Antonio Sánchez in 1779. Years of effort were put into the study of this manuscript by the great Spanish scholar Menéndez Pidal. By the use of chemical reagents he was able to resolve many problems relating to the reading of the difficult manuscript, but according to the late John Van Horne the manuscript was damaged in the process, so that further critical editions must depend upon somewhat incomplete photostatic records made during the course of Menéndez Pidal's research.

Several sheets of Per Abat's manuscript are missing, but the events which had been treated in the lost portions have been included as they appear in corresponding sections of later prose chronicles into which *The Cid* was incorporated. In the present translation these interpolated sections are enclosed in brackets.

Considerations of consistency have not been a binding factor in the rendering of proper names; in some cases the old Spanish form is used, and in others the modern Spanish, the choice being made on a purely arbitrary basis. The English form is used if a sufficiently familiar one exists; for example, "Saint Mary" denotes the person, "Santa María" the church.

To those readers who like to approximate a pronunciation of proper names this note is addressed: The written accent marks the vowel of the stressed syllable (*Gó*mez, Garc*í*a); names not bearing a written accent are stressed on the next-to-the-last syllable if the last letter is a vowel or *n* or *s* (Jim*e*na, R*o*drigo, Es*te*ban, *Vi*das), and on the last syllable if the last letter is any consonant other than *n* or *s* (Gus*ti*oz, Campea-*dor*). A syllable may contain a single vowel, or it may consist of *u* or *i*, unmarked by a written accent, plus another vowel

(Va-len-cia). The character ñ is equivalent orthographically to English *ny* (Fáñez); the diagraph *ll* represents the sound sometimes spelled *ly* in English (Téllez).

The text on which this translation is based is that of Ramón Menéndez Pidal, contained in *Cantar de mío Cid:* Texto, Gramática, y Vocabulario, Espasa Calpe, Madrid, tercera edición (rev. 1954). In only a few instances have I had the temerity to depart from his interpretations; almost all the notes which accompany this translation are derived from Don Ramón's work, itself a virtual epic of scholarship.

J. G. M.

THE EPIC OF THE CID

✒ I ✑

THE CID'S EXILE

[King Don Alfonso [1] sent the Cid Ruy Díaz to collect the tribute which the King of Córdoba and the King of Seville were obliged to pay him yearly. Almutamiz, the King of Seville, and Almudafar, the King of Granada, were at that time bitter enemies and hated each other vehemently. In the camp of Almudafar of Granada were the following noblemen: Count García Ordóñez, Fortún Sánchez, son-in-law of King Don García of Navarre, his brother Lope Sánchez, and Don Diego Pérez, one of the best knights of Castile.

Supported by the forces of all these noblemen, Almudafar marched against Almutamiz, the King of Seville.

When the Cid Ruy Díaz learned that they were coming to attack the King of Seville, who was a vassal and tributary of King Don Alfonso his lord, he viewed the situation darkly and was greatly disturbed. So to all of them he sent letters begging them, in consideration of the fealty owed to King Alfonso, not to march against the King of Seville nor to lay waste his lands. He warned them that if they insisted on going ahead, King Alfonso would not fail to come to the support of one who was his vassal and tributary. The King of Granada and the noblemen paid no heed whatever to the Cid's letters but made a fierce attack upon the King of Seville, laying waste the whole countryside and destroying the castle of Cabra.

Thereupon the Cid Ruy Díaz gathered together all the forces he could, Christians and Moors alike, and marched against the King of Granada in order to drive him from the land of the King of Seville. When they learned of the Cid's action, the King of Granada and his noblemen sent him

1 Several pages of Per Abat's manuscript are missing. The material in this bracketed section, and in those following, is supplied from corresponding sections of later prose chronicles. (See also the Note on the Text.)

word that his threats alone would never suffice to drive them from the country. Hearing this, the Cid decided that he would have to attack them. And so he did. He engaged them in a battle which lasted from early morning until midday. Great was the slaughter of both Moors and Christians who fought for the King of Granada. The Cid conquered them and drove them in flight from the battlefield. In this battle the Cid captured Count Don García Ordóñez and pulled a tuft of hair from his beard.[2] He also took prisoner many other knights—so many, in fact, that he lost count. The Cid kept them prisoner for three days and then set them free. During their captivity, he had his men collect the wealth of booty which lay abandoned on the field of battle. Then he and his company rejoined Almutamiz, the King of Seville. He gave back to the Moorish King and his followers every item of booty which they recognized as their own—and even anything they wanted which had not belonged to them originally.

And from that time on, Ruy Díaz was called by Moors and Christians alike the *Cid Campeador,* which means "Sir Champion."

Almutamiz then gave him many fine gifts and the tribute which he had come to collect. And the Cid returned with all the tribute to his lord King Alfonso. The King received him well, highly pleased with him and with everything he had done. For this reason many in the royal court became jealous of the Cid and by means of intrigue turned the will of the King against him.

---

[2] Laying hand to another man's beard was far more than a mere impertinence: it was a profound offense and an insult to his manhood. The beard was a symbol of manliness; and in the poem it is used metaphorically to denote the person of the knight. It was a common medieval custom to swear an oath by the beard. The epithet "he of the long beard" refers to an oath which the Cid made not to trim his beard as long as he remained an exile from Castile. The Cid binds his beard with a cord when he appears at the court seeking redress for the wrong done to his daughters, partly as a defiant token of his violated honor but more as a means of making it more difficult for his enemies to pull his beard. As I understand it, the Cid wound a cord or ribbon around his beard in such a way that it was completely covered.

The King was only too willing to listen to them, for he bore a grudge against the Cid. So he sent a letter to the Cid ordering him into exile. The Cid read the letter and, although he was filled with great sorrow, he decided to comply with the order at once, for he had been given only nine days to leave the country.

1

He summoned together his kinsmen and his vassals to tell them that he was under orders of the King to leave the kingdom within nine days; he inquired which of them were willing to accompany him into exile and which ones preferred to remain.

"May God reward those of you who go with me, and let me depart a friend of those who choose to stay behind."

Then spoke Álvar Fáñez, a cousin of the Cid, "We shall all go with you, Cid, through wilderness or through the haunts of men. We swear never to fail you as long as we have a last measure of life and strength. All our resources—mules, horses, money, clothing—shall we devote to your services. We shall always serve you as your loyal friends and vassals."

Immediately the others voiced their agreement with what Álvar Fáñez had said, and the Cid thanked them for their pledge.

Then the Cid set out from Vivar [3] on the road to Burgos, leaving empty and deserted the buildings of his estate.] [4]

Tears formed in the man's eyes as he turned his head for a final view of the estate. He saw doors swinging open, without locks; empty racks, where in former times hung furs and cloaks; empty perches, where once his falcons and his molting hunting hawks rested. The Cid, laden with sorrows, sighed deeply, and gravely spoke, "O almighty God on high! To this sad state have my wicked enemies brought me!"

[3] Vivar was the Cid's birthplace, a village about six miles north of the city of Burgos, where his estates were located.

[4] At this point, the second page of the manuscript, begins the text.

2

Thereupon they rode off, giving free rein to their horses. As they were leaving Vivar they saw a crow on the right; and yet as they were riding into Burgos they saw another on the left.[5] The Cid shrugged his shoulders and shook his head. "A good omen, Álvar Fáñez, for although we have been driven from Castile, we shall return in great honor."

3

The Cid Ruy Díaz entered Burgos; the pennants of sixty knights followed him. All the men and women of the town came out to see him; they appeared at the windows, weeping in sorrow, and the same lament came from the mouths of all:

"O God, what a noble vassal! Would only that he had a worthy lord to serve!"

4

How gladly would they have given him food and lodging! But no one dared incur the awesome wrath of King Don Alfonso. The evening before, the King's edict had been brought to Burgos, bearing the royal seal and containing stern orders that no one should extend hospitality to the Cid Ruy Díaz, and warning that whoever should do so would without fail lose his possessions and the eyes from his head—indeed his very soul and body. Great was the grief of all, and they kept out of the sight of the Cid, for they dared not even speak to him.

When the Campeador went to a house to secure lodging, he found the door strongly barred, a measure taken in fear of King Alfonso; if the door were ever to be opened to him, he would have to break it down. The men of the Cid's company

[5] The crow on the right was an omen of good fortune to come; the one on the left was a symbol of the misfortune the Cid had already suffered in being exiled from Castile.

began to call out, yet those inside would not answer. Then the Cid set spurs to his mount and rode up to the door; he pulled his foot from the stirrup and kicked on the door, but it was so securely bolted he could not open it.

A little girl of nine years came out and stood before the Cid. "O Campeador, God bless the hour you girt the sword! The King has forbidden us to help you. His edict came yesterday bearing the royal seal and the strictest orders. We dare not open our doors to you, nor take you in, for if we did, we would lose our homes and all we own—indeed the very eyes from our faces. O Cid, what will you gain if you harm us? May God protect you with His holy grace!"

Speaking thus, the little girl went back into her house.

Now the Cid saw clearly how little favor he might expect from the King.[6] He withdrew from the door and continued on his way through Burgos. Arriving at the church of Santa María, he dismounted and offered a devout prayer on bended knees. His prayer finished, he rode on, out through the gates of Santa María and across the river Arlanzón. Near the town of Burgos he had his tent pitched on a barren, sandy campsite, and then got off his horse. Thus, with a goodly number of followers, the Cid Ruy Díaz, who girt the sword in a blessed hour, had to camp in that rough spot as though he were far from civilization, for no one would give him shelter. He had been forbidden to buy provisions of any sort in the town of Burgos; the people dared not sell him a single day's provisions for even one man.

5

Martín Antolínez, that worthy man of Burgos, supplied the Cid and his men with food and wine. Since he had bought nothing—everything had come from his own stores—he was

---

[6] Banishment was usually accompanied by confiscation of property. The vassals of the expatriate were expected to follow him into exile, as did many of the Cid's, although in the poem they were not held to this obligation. The Cid of history was banished in 1081.

able to provide for their needs without disobeying the King. The noble Cid and the men in his service were highly gratified.

Then Martín Antolínez spoke as follows: "O Cid, God bless the hour you were born! Let us remain here for the night only, then leave at dawn. For I shall be reported for the service I have done you, and the displeasure of King Alfonso will fall upon me. If I join you in flight and escape with my life and health, sooner or later the King will allow me to return as a friend. But if he does not, I care hardly a fig for all I leave behind."

6

The Cid, who girt the sword in a blessed hour, spoke, "Martín Antolínez, O valiant knight, if I live I shall doubly reward your services. I have spent all my gold and silver; you can clearly see that I have brought nothing with me, and the needs of my company are great. Since no one will supply these needs voluntarily, I shall do so by force. If the idea seems good to you, I want two chests built. We shall fill them with sand, so that they will be very heavy. They are to be covered with tooled leather and wrought with ornamental studs.

7

"The leather will be scarlet, the nailwork gilded. Then bring Raquel and Vidas to me at once.[7] 'The King's anger has fallen on me, and the people of Burgos are forbidden to sell me anything,' I shall say to them. 'Since my treasure is too heavy to take with me, I wish to place it in pawn with you at a reasonable rate.' Have them come and take it away at night

[7] Nowhere in the poem is mentioned the fact that the usurers Raquel and Vidas are Jews. This tale of deception by means of sand-filled chests appears to belong to the stock of folklore and is typical of those contained in numerous medieval collections. *Disciplina clericalis*, a collection of apologues made by Petrus Alphonsus in the early part of the twelfth century, contains a similar tale.

so that not a living soul will see the deed. Let the Creator and all his saints bear witness that I am forced to use deception and that I do so against my will."

8

Straightway Martín Antolínez set out. He rode on through Burgos and entered the dwelling of Raquel and Vidas, where he made known his urgent desire to see them.

9

Raquel and Vidas were together, reckoning the profits from their dealings, when the wily Martín Antolínez entered.

"Hail, Raquel and Vidas, my dear friends. I should like to speak to both of you in private."

At once the three withdrew.

"Raquel and Vidas, give me your hands as a pledge that you will disclose this matter of mine to neither Moor nor Christian.[8] I am going to make you so rich that you will never want for anything. The Campeador went to collect tributes and came into possession of great and extraordinary riches. He kept back for himself everything of value, and he has been called to answer for his actions. He has two chests of very fine gold. You will understand, then, why the King is angry with him. The Cid has left his hereditary estate, his houses, and his palaces. He cannot take these chests of gold with him, for they would reveal what he has done. The Campeador pro-

---

[8] That the expression "neither Moor nor Christian" should come to be used with hardly more meaning than "no one at all" reflects the political and social situation in Spain during the eleventh century. The invaders had been living in Spain for nearly four centuries, and by this time a sort of uneasy adjustment between them and the Spaniards had been effected. Moor and Christian were frequently allied in campaigns against either Moor or Christian. Abengalbón, Moorish lord of Molina, was a great friend of the Cid and on several occasions provided lodging and an armed escort for the Cid's people. The Cid himself fought both with and against Moors and Christians, wherever the opportunity for booty might lie.

poses to leave the chests in your hands, and he wants you to
lend him a reasonable amount of money. Take the chests and
put them in your safekeeping. But both of you must swear a
mighty oath and give your word of honor that you will not
look into the chests for a year."

Raquel and Vidas conferred about the matter. "We have to
make a little profit from every venture. Surely the Cid must
have money, considering the great amount of wealth he
brought back from his raid on the land of the Moors. But a
person who travels with a large sum of money sleeps restlessly.
Let us take these two chests and hide them some place so
that no one can learn what the Cid has done."

"But tell us," they asked Martín Antolínez, "how much
money will the Cid want? How much interest will he pay us
for the whole year?"

Replied the astute Martín Antolínez, "The Cid will want
only what is just; he will ask for little, if only he may leave
his money in safety with you. Men from everywhere have im-
poverished themselves by abandoning their family estates to
join the Cid, and he needs six hundred marks."

Said Raquel and Vidas, "We are quite willing to furnish
him that amount."

"As you see, the night is coming on, and the Cid has no
time to lose. It is urgent that you give us the money at once."

Cried Raquel and Vidas, "That is not the way business is
done! First, we must have the chests, and then we shall give
you the money."

"Of course," replied Martín Antolínez. "Come to the camp
of the famed Campeador, and we shall help you, as is no more
than right, to bring the chests here and place them in your
safekeeping so that neither Moor nor Christian will ever find
out what has been done."

" 'Tis a bargain," said Raquel and Vidas. "When the chests
have been delivered, you will get your six hundred marks."

Martín Antolínez quickly set out on horseback with the
eager Raquel and Vidas. They forded the river instead of

using the bridge so that not a living soul from Burgos might see them. Arriving at the tent of the honored Campeador, they entered and kissed his hand. The Cid greeted Raquel and Vidas with a smile and rebuked them gently because they had not come to see him in such a long time.

"The King's displeasure drives me from my country," he told them. "I believe that you are to have a share of my wealth. You shall never be in want as long as you live."

Raquel and Vidas kissed the Cid's hands. Martín Antolínez completed the arrangements whereby they were to give the Cid six hundred marks on the security of the chests; the latter were to be kept in safety for him for one year. They gave their pledge and they swore not to open them within this time; if they should break their word, the Cid was not to give them one wretched cent of interest on the loan.

Spoke Martín Antolínez, "Let the chests be loaded now. Take them with you, Raquel and Vidas, and put them in safekeeping. I shall go with you in order to bring back the marks. The Cid must be on the march before the cock crows tomorrow."

What a delightful surprise was theirs as they loaded the chests! For although they were a strong pair, they were unable to lift them by themselves to the backs of the mules. Raquel and Vidas were overjoyed with the treasure they believed to be minted gold, and they thought they were getting enough to make them rich for the rest of their days.

10

Raquel kissed the Cid's hand and said, "O Campeador, God bless the day you girt the sword! You are leaving Castile for strange lands. Wondrous is your good fortune, and great is your wealth. O Cid, let me have, I beg of you, a beautiful Moorish robe of scarlet for a gift." [9]

9 In financial transactions it was customary for one party to make the other a gift of some article of clothing or the equivalent in money. For

"Very well," said the Cid, "it shall be given to you, and if I do not bring it back from the land of the Moors, then you may charge the cost of it against what you find in the chests."

Raquel and Vidas departed with the chests, and Martín Antolínez went with them into Burgos. With all caution, they approached their house. In the main hall a fine, white linen cloth was spread over a small carpet. Immediately, they put down upon it three hundred silver marks which Don Martín counted and accepted without weighing. Another three hundred marks were paid in gold. Don Martín turned the money over to the five squires he had brought with him. Then he said, "The chests, Don Raquel and Don Vidas, are in your hands. I should think I deserve a gift for the profit I have turned your way."

11

Raquel and Vidas drew aside for a moment. "Let us give him a fine gift, for he is the one who has brought us this piece of business.

"O honored Martín Antolínez of Burgos, we are going to give you a splendid gift, for you deserve it fully. Here are thirty marks; have yourself made a pair of breeches, a fine cloak, and a costly mantle. You will further earn it, for it is your duty to see that our agreement is carried out."

As he accepted the money, Don Martín thanked them, bade them farewell, and left the house. Out of Burgos he rode, across the Arlanzón, and up to the tent of the hero born under a favorable star.

The Cid received him with arms outstretched. "You have come back, Martín Antolínez, my faithful vassal! May I yet live to see the day when I shall reward you."

"I have returned, O Campeador, and I come with good news. I have obtained six hundred marks for you and thirty more

---

his part in arranging the loan, Martín Antolínez will ask Raquel and Vidas for such a gift and will receive thirty marks with which to buy clothing.

for myself.[10] Give the order to strike camp, and let us be off at once so that we may be in San Pedro de Cardeña when the cock crows. There we shall see your noble and virtuous lady. But we must stay only briefly, and then cross the border, for our final day of grace draws near."

12

When he finished speaking, they broke camp, and the Cid and his company rode off at once. The Cid turned his horse's head toward the Cathedral of Santa María, and, making the sign of the cross with his right hand, said, "O God, who ruleth heaven and earth, I thank thee. Aid me, O holy Mother of God, with thy might! Now the displeasure of the King drives me from Castile, and I do not know if I shall ever live to see my land again. Protect me by thy grace, O Mother of glory, as I depart. Strengthen me and be with me by night and by day. If thou grant my prayer, and if good fortune follows me, I shall offer fine and costly gifts at thine altar, and I promise thee a thousand masses will be sung before it."

13

Thus the Cid made his solemn farewell. Then they all gave their horses free rein and rode away. Said that loyal knight of Burgos, Martín Antolínez, "I must have time to go see my wife and arrange for the management of the household in my

[10] We never learn whether or not the Cid repaid the loan. However, Minaya Álvar Fáñez, when he goes to Castile to bring the Cid's wife and daughters to Valencia (section 83), meets Raquel and Vidas and promises to speak to the Cid about payment of the debt, giving them to hope that they will be richly rewarded. Considering the customary generosity of the Cid toward his king and his vassals, we can assume that he repaid this relatively small debt. Nevertheless, since they were Jews, there would be no dishonor attached to cheating them. Historically, it is not likely that he really pulled this trick, nor does it seem plausible that Raquel and Vidas should be so gullible as to be taken in by it.

absence. Let the King take everything I possess if he likes; I do not care. I shall be back to join you before sunrise."

14

Don Martín returned to Burgos, while the Cid made his way as fast as he could ride toward the monastery of San Pedro de Cardeña, and with him those knights who duly served him. Soon the cocks began to crow, and the first signs of day were appearing when the noble Campeador reached San Pedro. As dawn broke, that holy servant of God, Abbot Don Sancho, was saying his morning prayers. Doña Jimena, attended by five worthy ladies in waiting, was praying to Saint Peter and the Creator, "O thou who guidest the lives of all, watch over my Cid Campeador!"

15

The Cid's party knocked at the door, and the call was heard within. O Lord, what pleasure Abbot Don Sancho showed! Carrying torches and candles, the monks all poured out into the courtyard to give a jubilant reception to the hero born in a blessed hour.

"Thanks be to God," cried Abbot Don Sancho, "for your arrival! The hospitality of this house is yours."

Replied the Cid, born in a blessed hour, "My thanks, worthy Abbot; I am pleased by your kindness. I shall get food for myself and for my vassals.

"I am leaving the country and I want to give you fifty marks; if I live, you will some day see this sum doubled. Since I do not wish to put your monastery to any expense, I am giving you a hundred marks more to shelter Doña Jimena and her daughters and their ladies during the year.[11] In your

11 The monastery of San Pedro de Cardeña, as well as the Abbot himself, had been the object of the Cid's beneficence and protection before his exile, and he could be sure that he was leaving his wife and daughters in safe hands.

trust, Abbot Don Sancho, I leave my two little daughters; attend them and my wife with all heed. If this money should be too meager to supply their needs, spare no expense, I charge you, and I promise to repay fourfold to the monastery every mark you spend."

The Abbot declared that he would gladly comply with the Cid's request.

Now Doña Jimena appeared before the Cid, followed by ladies in waiting who were carrying her two daughters in their arms. Doña Jimena knelt before the Campeador; tears came to her eyes as she kissed his hands.

"O Campeador, born in a blessed hour! Evil plotters have driven you from your land.

16

"Hear me, O Cid of the noble beard! Here before you am I with your daughters, little ones of tender age, and with my ladies who serve me. You are to depart, and we must be separated from you. Tell us, for the love of Saint Mary, what are we to do?"

He of the noble beard reached out his arms and took into them his little daughters, holding them close to his heart with deep affection. Tears came to his eyes, and he sighed. "O Doña Jimena, my wonderful wife, I love you more than my very soul. The hour of parting has come; I must go away and leave you here. May God and Saint Mary yet grant me to see the day when I may give these daughters of mine in marriage; may I live to see such fortune and to serve you again, my honored wife."

17

A mighty repast was spread for the noble Campeador, and loudly the bells of San Pedro pealed out.

Throughout Castile ran the report of the Cid Campeador's banishment. To follow him, men gave up their homes and estates. That very day, a hundred and fifteen knights gathered at the bridge on the Arlanzón, inquiring the whereabouts of the Cid Campeador. Joined by Martín Antolínez, they went to meet the Cid at the monastery of San Pedro.

18

When the Cid Rodrigo de Vivar got word of this addition to his forces, whereby his prestige was also increased, he rode out at once to meet the newcomers. As he came within sight of them, he smiled. Then each one approached and kissed his hand in token of vassalage. With great feeling the Cid addressed them, "I pray our God and Spiritual Father that before I die I may be able to repay you, who have abandoned your homes and estates in order to join me. What you have lost you shall regain twofold."

The Cid rejoiced greatly to see his forces increased, and all his men rejoiced with him.

Six days had now come and gone since sentence of banishment was imposed on the Cid; three days, and only three, remained in which to comply with the order. The King had ordered a close watch to be kept on the Cid; if he should be caught in the country after the ninth day, no amount of gold or silver would buy his freedom.

As daylight waned and evening fell, the Campeador bade his men gather about him.

"Hear me, O knights, and do not fall into despair. Although I have very little money with me, yet each one of you shall have a share. Heed well what you are to do: When the cocks crow tomorrow morning, you will have your horses saddled without delay. In San Pedro the good Abbot will call us to morning prayers, and there he will say for us the Mass of the Holy Trinity. After that, let us take to the saddle, for the end of the allotted time is drawing near, and a long ride is before us."

Everyone did what the Cid had ordered. Night passed, and morning drew near. Before the light of day, they began to saddle their horses. The morning bells rang out their urgent call to prayers, and the Cid and his lady made their way to the church. Doña Jimena knelt on the steps before the altar and prayed with all her soul that the Creator might protect the Cid Campeador from harm.

"O Lord of glory, O Father who art in heaven! Thou who hast created the heavens and the earth and the sea, Thou who hast made the stars and the moon and the warmth-giving sun!

"O Thou, incarnate in Mother Saint Mary, born in Bethlehem at Thy divine will, where shepherds did glorify Thee and praise Thee, and whither did come three kings of Arabia to adore Thee, Melchior, Caspar, and Balthasar, offering Thee from their hearts their gifts of gold, frankincense, and myrrh.

"Thou didst rescue Jonah when he fell into the sea, and Thou didst save Daniel from death in that infamous den of lions, and Thou didst save Saint Sebastian in Rome, and likewise didst Thou deliver Saint Susanna from false witness.

"Thou didst walk upon the earth for thirty-two years, O Spiritual Lord, working miracles of wide renown. Thou didst turn water into wine and stone into bread. At Thy will Thou didst raise up Lazarus from the dead.

"Thou didst suffer the Jews to seize Thee and to set Thee on a cross atop Mount Calvary in a place named Golgotha. And with Thee were crucified two thieves, one on the right hand and the other on the left, and one of them did enter paradise, while the other entered not. Even on the cross didst Thou perform a wondrous miracle: Blind Longinus, sightless all his life, did cast his spear into Thy side; Thy spilled blood ran down the shaft, staining his hands; when he touched them to his face, he opened his eyes and had the power to see around him; at once he did believe in Thee and was saved from evil.

"Thou didst rise from the tomb and of Thine own will didst descend to hell, burst open its doors, and bring forth from limbo the souls of the saintly patriarchs.

"Thou art King of Kings and Father of all the world. I

adore Thee and believe in Thee with all my heart. May Saint Peter support my prayers for the Cid Campeador; God keep him from harm, and may we who part today meet again in this life."

Her prayer finished and the mass sung, they leave the church, and the knights begin to mount their horses. The Cid embraces Doña Jimena, and she kisses his hand, weeping and distraught. He turns his eyes upon his daughters.

"To the care of God the Heavenly Father I entrust you, for only he knows when we who part shall see each other again."

Never before was seen such grief; the pain of their parting is like the tearing of a nail from the finger.

The Cid and his men begin to ride off, but he falls behind and keeps turning his head to look back. Then Minaya Álvar Fáñez offers some timely reassurance. "Courage, O Cid, born of woman in a blessed hour! Let us be on our way and have done with parting. All this sorrow will at last turn to joy, for God will give us a guiding hand, even as he has given us a soul."

Again, the Abbot Don Sancho is charged to look well to the care of Doña Jimena and her children, as well as of the ladies who serve them, and he is assured that he will be richly rewarded for his services.

Don Sancho turns to Álvar Fáñez, who speaks to him, "If men come along seeking to join us, tell them, Abbot, to follow our trail and ride hard, and they will come upon us either in some town or in the open country."

They gave their horses rein and rode off, for the time was drawing near when they had to be out of the kingdom.

The Cid halted that night in Espinazo de Can, where great numbers came from all parts of the land to join his band. Next morning, on they rode. His route into exile took the loyal-hearted Cid to the left of that fine city, San Esteban, and through Alcubilla near the border of Castile; he crossed the Quinea highroad, and then at Navapalos he passed over

the river Duero, making camp for the night at Figueruela.
Along the way, men from everywhere kept coming to join him.

19

That night, when the Cid lay down, a sweet slumber came
over him, and he fell into a sound sleep. The Archangel
Gabriel appeared to him in a vision with these words: "Ride
on, O noble Cid Campeador; never before has any knight rid-
den with brighter fortune than shall be thine. Success will ride
with thee as long as thou shalt live."

When the Cid awoke, he made the sign of the cross.

20

After crossing himself, he placed his fate in God's hands,
feeling his spirits lifted by his dream. The next morning they
took to their horses again, for this was the last day of the Cid's
allotted time. They ended the day's ride at the Sierra de
Miedes. On the left stood the towers of Atienza, at that time
in the hands of the Moors.

21

It was still daylight, for the sun had not yet gone down. The
Cid ordered his forces to form and pass in review. In addition
to the valiant troops of foot soldiers, he counted the lances of
three hundred knights, and on each lance waved a pennant.

22

"God save you, my knights! Early in the morning feed your
horses their grain. Those of you who want to eat are to do so;
those who do not will mount up. We shall cross the mountain
range, rough and towering, and tonight we shall leave King
Alfonso's realm behind us. If any wish to join us, there they
can find us."

Through the night they made their way up to the divide, and at daybreak they started down the slope. In a large and beautiful wooded area the Cid ordered a halt so that the horses could be fed. He informed his men of his desire to travel by night, and, as befits good vassals, they agreed, ready to carry out the orders of their lord.

Before nightfall they resumed their ride, traveling by night so that no one might learn their movements. They pressed on all night without halting for rest. Near the town of Castejón on the river Henares, the Cid deployed his forces in ambush.

23

At the suggestion of Minaya Álvar Fáñez, the Cid lay in concealment all night long. It was Minaya, also, who counseled as follows: "O Cid, God bless the hour you girt the sword! After we have drawn the people of Castejón into our trap and taken the place, I propose that you remain behind to secure it with a hundred of our knights. Give me two hundred to take out to forage for supplies. With your good luck and God's help it will be a profitable venture for us."

Said the Campeador, "You have spoken well, Minaya. You shall go with the two hundred men on this raid you propose. With you will go Álvar Álvarez, and the peerless knight, Álvar Salvadórez, and the mighty lance of Galindo García. There will be brave men in your party, Minaya. Strike boldly, and do not let caution keep you from taking spoils. Take your foragers down to Hita and through Guadalajara, then on to Alcalá. Take all the plunder you can, and leave nothing out of fear of the Moors. With one hundred knights I shall remain behind and hold Castejón, for the place will serve well as our stronghold. Should you meet some misfortune on the raid, just send word back to me at once, and all Spain will talk of the way I came to your aid."

Then they called out the names of those who were to go on the raid and those who would stay behind with the Cid.

The sky was beginning to lighten and dawn was drawing near; now the sun began to rise in glorious beauty. The people of Castejón left their beds, and were going out to their work in the fields. Most of them were outside the walls now, the gates left open; very few remained in Castejón, and those without the walls had scattered in all directions.

Now the Cid Campeador and his men came out of hiding and surrounded Castejón. Moorish men and women were captured as booty, and all the herds in the vicinity were taken. The Cid Don Rodrigo swept up to the gate; the guards were terrorized by the surprise assault and fled their posts. With his naked sword in his hand the Cid Ruy Díaz passed through the gate and slew fifteen Moors who fell within his reach.

Castejón had fallen to him, and its wealth of gold and silver was his. His knights came bringing in the plunder, and, setting little value on the prize, gave it to the Cid.

Meanwhile, the two hundred and three men of the raiding party rode boldly, plundering the countryside as they went. Minaya's standard advanced to Alcalá de Henares; from there the band turned back with their plunder up the river Henares and through Guadalajara. Great was the booty they had taken: sheep and cattle, raiment, and other costly objects. Minaya's pennant continued unimpeded, for no one was rash enough to assault it from the rear. With the riches they had won, the band held a straight course back to Castejón and the Cid.

As the raiders neared the town, the Campeador and his men left the stronghold under guard and rode out to meet Minaya. The Cid received him with open arms. "Welcome, Álvar Fáñez, valiant knight! Whatever mission I entrust to you is certain to succeed. The booty you have won, Minaya, shall be added to mine, and I shall give you a fifth of the whole, if you will have it." [12]

[12] The Cid had the right to collect a fifth (sometimes a smaller amount) of all booty his vassals might win in war, just as the Cid would be bound to give a fifth to his King, Alfonso VI, if he were not in exile.

24

"O illustrious Campeador, I thank you. The fifth part which you have promised me would delight even Alfonso, King of Castile. But I release you from your offer; keep the treasure. I swear to God on high that never will I accept a single coin from you until I have had my fill of doing battle against the Moors on my noble steed, of wielding the lance and the sword until my arm drips blood to the elbow, fighting under the banner of the Cid Ruy Díaz, the peerless champion. Not until I shall have helped you win some prize of real worth will I take a share; keep, then, these riches for your own."

25

The booty was all collected. Now the Cid, who girt the sword in a blessed hour, realized that Alfonso might hear of their activities and proceed with hostile intent against him and his followers. He detailed certain ones to divide all the plunder and to give him a record of what each had received. The knights saw their fortunes mount, for each one got a hundred silver marks; half that amount was the share of each infantryman; as was the usual case, the Cid kept a fifth of the whole. But he could not sell his booty in Castejón, nor was there anyone in that place to whom he wished to give it as a gift; neither did he want to encumber his movements with captives. So, after talking to the people of Castejón, he sent word to Hita and Guadalajara that his share of the booty could be bought for so little that there would be great profit for the purchasers. The Moors bid three thousand silver marks, an offer which the Cid considered acceptable, and three days later the money was duly paid to him.

The Cid decided that he could not quarter his men in the fortress, for the water supply was inadequate; otherwise, he would have retained possession of it. Since the Moors he had defeated were living under a treaty of peace with King Alfonso, the Cid feared that the King would come to take strong measures of reprisal.

"Hear me, O Minaya, hear me, O knights! I have decided to withdraw from Castejón.

26

"Do not be downcast by what I am going to tell you. We cannot remain in Castejón, for King Alfonso is not far away and may come to attack us. And yet I do not want to destroy this fortress. Let us set free a hundred men and a hundred women of the Moors we hold captive so that there will be no complaints about our taking their goods as spoils. All of you have profited, not one man excepted. Tomorrow morning, then, let us make ready to leave, for I should not wish to enter the field of battle against my lord Alfonso." [13]

All were pleased with the Cid's words. Loaded with spoils, they left the castle they had taken, and the Moors—men and women alike—called out their blessings on the Cid.

They went up the river Henares as far as they could, and on through Alcarria, and past the caves of Anguita; crossing the river Tajuña, they entered the plains of Taranz and pressed on toward the far edge of that region. Having taken a great amount of plunder as he passed through the countryside, the Cid stopped to camp between Ariza and Cetina. The Moors did not perceive the bold intentions of this band of men.

The next day the Cid broke camp; his route that day took him through Alhama, La Hoz, Briviesca, and on to Ateca. Near Alcocer he halted his company on a large, round hill, a strong position which could not be cut off from water, for the

---

[13] Despite the treatment he received at the hands of King Alfonso, the Cid in numerous instances shows himself to be loyal, deferent, and even obsequious toward his King. The Cid had the right as an exile to raid the lands of King Alfonso and those under his protection, but those who had voluntarily joined him in exile did not.

river Jalón ran nearby. The Cid Don Rodrigo planned to
seize the castle of Alcocer.

27

On this elevated ground he built camp, strategically plac-
ing some of his tents on the side of the hill and others toward
the river. The noble Campeador, who girt the sword in a
blessed hour, ordered his men to dig a trench around the hill
and along the river, so that they would be protected day and
night against surprise attack. "Let all men be aware," he de-
clared, "that the Cid is encamped here and here intends to
stay."

28

Throughout that part of the country spread the news that
the Cid Campeador lay encamped there and that he had left
Christian territory to live in the land of the Moors. None of
the Moorish farmers dared work the fields which lay near the
camp. The Cid and his men rejoiced that the castle of Alcocer
was paying them tribute.

29

The people of Alcocer would soon be paying tribute to the
Cid; he was also receiving it from the towns of Ateca, Terrer,
and Calatayud, although the people of Calatayud paid their
tribute grudgingly.

The Cid maintained the siege against Alcocer for fifteen full
weeks.

When the Cid perceived that Alcocer was not going to sur-
render to him, he contrived a stratagem which he carried out
at once. He struck all the tents except one and marched his
band off downstream along the Jalón, his banner flying, his
knights in armor and girt with sword. The plan was to draw

the people from the walls of Alcocer into an ambush. How the latter rejoiced at what they saw!

"The Cid's supplies of bread and grain are exhausted," they reasoned. "He has moved all but one of his tents and now withdraws as though in utter rout. Let us attack him and we shall win much booty. But there must be no delay, for if those people of Terrer take the Cid before we do, we are sure to get none of the spoils they capture. We shall make him return twice over the tribute he has taken from us."

Then out from Alcocer the townsmen poured in a headlong rush.

When the Cid saw them outside the fortress, he pretended to flee, heading down the river Jalón with his ranks in disorder.

"Our prize is getting away from us!" cried the people of Alcocer.

Old and young came running from Alcocer, driven by the desire to catch the Cid and forgetting all else. Behind them they left the gates wide open and unguarded.

The mighty Campeador turned to look back, and seeing how far his pursuers were from the protection of the fortress, he ordered an about face. His knights set spur to horse.

"Attack, brave knights! By the grace of God, the prize will be ours."

The battle was joined in the midst of the plain. O Lord, how high their spirits ran that morning! In the van rode the Cid and Álvar Fáñez on their strong and well-trained steeds. Quickly, they cut the Moors off from the castle. The Cid's vassals struck without mercy, and in a short time they had killed three hundred Moors. Those whom the Cid had stationed in ambush now appeared; making a great outcry, they advanced with naked swords on the fortress and assembled at the gateway. Soon they were joined by their comrades in arms, and the victory was won.

This, then, is the strategy by which the Cid took Alcocer.

30

Pedro Bermúdez rode up with the Cid's banner and fastened it to the very highest point of the fortress. Then spoke the Cid, born in a blessed hour, "Thanks be to God on high and to all his saints! Now both man and mount will have more fitting quarters.

31

"Hear me, O Álvar Fáñez, and all my knights! Along with this castle, we have taken great booty. Moors lie dead all about us and few are left alive. We cannot sell these men and women as slaves, and it would do us no good to cut off their heads. So, let us keep them inside the fortress, since now we are masters of the place; we shall lodge in their houses, and they will be our servants."

32

The Cid, established in the castle of Alcocer and in possession of all the booty, sent for the tent which he had left in camp.

His triumph sorely vexed the men of Ateca, nor was it borne well by those of Terrer and Calatayud. They sent the following message to the King of Valencia: [14] "A knight called the Cid Ruy Díaz de Vivar, whom King Alfonso banished from his land in disfavor, has set a close siege to Alcocer. By a ruse he has drawn the people into his ambush and has captured the castle. If you do not come to our aid, you will lose Ateca and Terrer, nor will Calatayud escape the same fate; the situation will be equally precarious along the river Jalón, as well as on the river Jaloca in the other direction."

When King Tamín of Valencia received this report he be-

[14] Valencia was in Moorish hands at the time, as, of course, was more than half of Spain, including the area in which the Cid is campaigning at this point in the narrative.

came alarmed and angered. "Here before me are three Moorish emirs.[15] Two of you will go there at once with three thousand Moorish warriors, fully armed. With the help of those on the border you will capture this man alive and bring him back to me. He is going to answer to me for this invasion of my territory."

Three thousand Moors mounted and set out, reaching Segorbe that night, where they rested. The next day's ride took them to Cella, where they again spent a night. There they sent for those along the borders, who straightway joined the main force from every side. They left Cella del Canal, as it is called, and after traveling all day without rest ended their journey at nightfall in Calatayud. The call went out through those lands, and men in countless numbers came to join these emirs, whose names were Fáriz and Galve. Their objective was to lay siege to the noble Cid in Alcocer.

33

The besieging host raised their tents and made camp. Already very numerous, they kept growing larger. Night and day the sentinels of the outposts, which the Moors had established around the castle, walked their posts in full armor. The outposts were everywhere; the encampment was enormous.

The Cid's men, since their supply of water had been cut off, were eager to go out to do battle, but he restrained them firmly.

The siege of the fortress continued for three weeks.

34

After three weeks and well into the fourth the Cid made a decision in conference with his men.

"The Moors have cut us off from our supply of water, and our provisions will soon be exhausted. If we try to escape by night, they will block us. Their forces are too numerous for

[15] Moorish military commanders.

us to attack. Tell me, my knights, what do you think we had best do?"

First spoke the illustrious knight Minaya: "We are living here in a hostile land, exiled from our stately Castile. Our only means of obtaining sustenance is to take it from the Moors in battle. There are six hundred of us, perhaps a few more. In the name of the Creator, let us not do otherwise than to go forth to battle, and let it be no later than tomorrow."

"You have spoken my own opinion," said the Campeador, "and your words have done you honor, as might well have been expected."

He had all the Moors, both men and women, sent outside the fortress, so that no one would discover his plans. His knights spent that day and the following night putting their weapons and armor in order. Before sunrise the next day the Cid and all his men were armed and ready.

The Cid spoke as follows: "Every one of us will take part in the sally except two foot soldiers who will stay to guard the gate. Only if we fall on the field of battle will they regain the castle. And if we defeat them we shall gain great riches. You, Pedro Bermúdez, shall bear my standard; I know you will guard it faithfully, my valiant knight. But you shall not advance it until I give you the order."

Pedro Bermúdez kissed the Cid's hand and took up the standard.

The gates swing open, and the forces of the Cid sally forth. The Moorish sentinels run back to report this development to their main forces. In frenzied haste the Moors set about donning their armor; the earth begins to tremble to the thunder of their battle drums; [16] everywhere Moors take up arms and fall swiftly into ranks. There are two principal banners in the Moorish army and countless pennants of lesser rank.

The Moorish battle lines move forward, closing upon those of the Cid.

[16] Moorish armies used drums for the purpose of terrifying their Christian enemies, and it is said to have had the intended effect, particularly on those who heard them for the first time.

"Hold your positions, my men!" orders the Cid. "No one is to advance until I give the command!"

But Pedro Bermúdez cannot restrain himself; raising the standard aloft, he strikes spurs to his horse. "The might of God be with you, O steadfast Campeador! I am going to carry your banner into the very thickest of the enemy ranks, and then we shall see how those who owe it fealty rally around."

Cries the Campeador, "No! No! For the love of heaven!"

Replies Pedro Bermúdez, "So be it, I say!" And he spurs into the densest ranks with the standard. He is met by the Moors, who try to capture the standard. Their fierce blows fall on him but fail to penetrate his armor.

The Cid shouts, "To his aid, for the love of heaven!"

35

Shields in front of their breasts, pennant-flying lances lowered into position, and bodies leaning forward over the saddle, the strong-hearted knights ride to the attack.

The battle cry of the Cid rings out: "Attack them, O knights, in the name of God! I am Ruy Díaz de Vivar, the Cid Campeador!"

They charge into the ranks where Pedro Bermúdez has carried the standard. Three hundred lances, all adorned with pennants, strike three hundred blows and kill an equal number of Moors. They withdraw and charge again, and another three hundred Moors are slain.

36

All over the battlefield lances are lowered and raised. Shields are penetrated and split, coats of mail cut to shreds. On hundreds of lances white pennants turn red with blood. Many a fine war horse runs about riderless. The Moors cry out the name of Mohammed; the Christians call upon Saint James.

In a short time a thousand and three hundred Moors lie
dead on the field.

37

Mighty is the combat waged by that skilled warrior the Cid
Ruy Díaz in his gilded saddle, and by Minaya Álvar Fáñez,
lord of Zurita; Martín Antolínez, renowned in Burgos, and
Muño Muñoz, reared in the Cid's own household,[17] fight
bravely, as do Martín Muñoz, lord of Monte Mayor, Álvar
Álvarez, and Álvar Salvadórez, and the noble Aragonese, Ga-
lindo García, and the Cid's nephew Félix Muñoz. To a man
they rally to the prompt support of the Cid Campeador and
his standard.

38

Minaya Álvar Fáñez has his horse cut down from under
him, and immediately the Christians rush to his aid. His lance
broken, he draws his sword and, although on foot, wields it
with telling effect. Seeing his vassal in peril, Ruy Díaz, the
Castilian, rides up to a well-mounted Moorish officer and tak-
ing his sword in his right hand, strikes him a blow at the waist
which cuts the Moor in two, so that half his body topples to
the ground. Then he leads the Moor's charger over to Minaya
Álvar Fáñez, saying, "To horse, Minaya; you are my right-
hand man, and I shall have great need of your support this
day. The Moors are still standing fast on the field, and we
must renew the attack."

Minaya, remounted, furiously fights his way through the
enemy, slaying with his sword all he meets.

The Cid Ruy Díaz, born in a blessed hour, strikes three

---

17 In the Middle Ages young boys, as well as girls, were frequently sent
to live in the home of a nobleman where they were reared and the boys
trained for knighthood. A complexity of duties and privileges character-
ized the relationship between the boy, or *criado*, and the lord. The two
daughters of the Cid were reared in the household of King Alfonso VI.

times at the Emir Fáriz; two of the blows have no effect, but the third strikes home, and blood splashes over the Moor's coat of mail. The latter wheels his horse and starts to flee from the battleground. With this blow of the sword the Cid has turned the tide of battle against the Moorish forces.

39

Martín Antolínez strikes Galve a blow which splits the Moorish Emir's helmet, knocking off the rubies adorning it. His head wounded, the Moor lacks the courage to wait for a second such blow. Now the Emirs Fáriz and Galve are vanquished. What a day for the Christians! Everywhere the Moors are put to flight, and the Cid's men pursue them and cut them down. The Emir Fáriz finds refuge in the village of Terrer, but the people there refuse to extend protection to Galve, who flees in desperate speed toward Calatayud. The Cid follows him at close range; the chase ends at Calatayud.

40

The horse taken from the Moor for Álvar Fáñez proved to be excellent, and the knight succeeded in killing thirty-four of the enemy. Keen-edged was his sword, and his arm was drenched to the elbow with Moorish blood. Said Minaya, "Now all is well, for the glorious news will reach Castile that the Cid has triumphed on the field of battle."

Many Moors lay dead, and the few survivors were pursued relentlessly. Later the Cid's forces turned back. The Cid, knight of destiny, sat astride his goodly steed, sword in hand, his hood of mail pushed back on his shoulders, the cloth cap folded back on his head. O Lord, how handsome was his beard! As he watched his men returning he cried, "Thanks be to God on high! What a great battle we have won!"

The Cid's men proceeded to strip the enemy camp of shields and other arms and all sorts of costly objects. When all the Moorish horses were rounded up they tallied five hundred and ten. Great was the rejoicing among the Christians when it was learned that only fifteen of their number had fallen. They brought in an almost incalculable sum of gold and silver. Those Christian knights were now made rich with the booty they had taken.

The Moors of Alcocer were allowed to return within the castle, and the Cid even directed that something should be given to each one of them.

Amid unanimous rejoicing the Cid gave the word to divide the money and other great riches. The fifth part due the leader included a hundred chargers. Splendid was the share he gave to each of his vassals, knight and foot soldier alike. The division of the spoils was so justly made by their leader, born in a blessed hour, that all his followers were more than satisfied.

Spoke the Cid: "Hear me, O Minaya, my strong right arm! From this God-sent wealth take all you want for yourself. Now, I wish to send you to Castile with the report of this battle we have won. To King Alfonso, whose disfavor has fallen upon me, I wish to send a gift of thirty war horses, each with a handsome saddle and bridle, and each with a sword slung from the saddlebow."

Replied Minaya Álvar Fáñez, "Gladly will I do so."

41

"Here is a boot filled to the top with fine gold and silver. In the Cathedral of Santa María have a thousand masses said; whatever is left over, give to my wife and my daughters. Bid them pray for me night and day. If I live, I shall yet make them wealthy ladies."

42

Minaya Álvar Fáñez welcomed the assignment. Men were detailed to accompany him, and the horses were given their grain. At nightfall the Cid called his knights to a council.

43

"Now, Minaya, you are to go to proud Castile. There you will tell our friends that God has availed us, and we have conquered on the field of battle. If you do not find us here when you return, follow us by reports of our whereabouts. We must live by the sword and the lance, for in no other way will this poor region support us, and I fear that we shall have to leave it."

44

The arrangements made, Minaya set out the next morning, and the Campeador remained in Alcocer with his men.

The soil in that region was extremely poor and unproductive.

The Moors along the border, as well as those from beyond, kept spying on the Cid's activities; they were plotting something with the Emir Fáriz, who had recovered from his wound.

But the people of Ateca and the town of Terrer and of the more splendid city of Calatayud made a written offer of three thousand silver marks for the stronghold of Alcocer, and the Cid sold it to them.

45

The Cid Ruy Díaz has sold Alcocer! He has given a generous share of the money to each of his vassals, enriching knight and foot soldier alike. In all his band there is not a single man in want. He prospers ever who serves a good lord.

46

When the Cid resolved to leave the castle, the Moors of Alcocer, men and women alike, were grieved. "Are you leaving us, O Cid?" they lamented. "Our grateful prayers will follow you, for you have treated us with justice."

And as the Cid left Alcocer, the Moors set up a wailing.

The Campeador raised his standard and departed, riding down the river Jalón. When he turned aside from the stream he saw birds of good omen.

While the people of Terrer were pleased at the Cid's departure, and those of Calatayud were even more so, yet the townsmen of Alcocer were grieved, for the Cid had treated them well.

The Cid rode on until he came to El Poyo, a prominence overlooking Monreal. El Poyo was lofty and quite large, secure on all sides from enemy attack.

First, the Cid subjected the town of Daroca to tribute, then Molina in the other direction, and farther on, Teruel; he also brought Cella del Canal into his possession.

47

May heaven ever lend grace to the Cid Ruy Díaz!

Minaya Álvar Fáñez reached Castile and presented the thirty horses to King Alfonso. When the King saw them, his face lit up with a smile. "God help you, Minaya, who has given me these?"

"My Cid Ruy Díaz, who girt the sword in a blessed hour. After he was exiled, he took the fortress of Alcocer by means of a stratagem. The King of Valencia sent a force to besiege Alcocer as soon as he learned of its capture. When they cut off his water supply, the Cid came out of the castle to engage the enemy in a battle in which he vanquished two Moorish emirs and won a great abundance of booty. To you, O honored King, he sends this gift. He kisses your hands and your feet in supplication of your favor, and he prays to God for heaven's blessings on you."

Spoke the King, "Only a short time ago he fell from favor and was exiled; it is too soon to return such a one to favor. But, since this gift comes to me at the expense of the Moors, I shall accept it. Moreover, the gains the Cid has made are gratifying to me. To you, Minaya, I give full pardon and restore to you your lands and offices. You may go and come as you wish, for I hereby grant you my favor. But as to the Cid, I shall not say a word.

48

"However, Álvar Fáñez, I wish to make it known to you that any good and valiant knight of my realm who so desires may go to join the Cid without penalty of person or property."

Minaya Álvar Fáñez kissed the King's hands and expressed the gratitude he felt toward the King, his lord by right of birth. "This much you have granted us today; in days to come, with the aid of God, we shall deserve to have our fullest wishes granted."

"Lose no more time with words, Minaya," replied the King. "Go without fear to rejoin the Cid, for no man in Castile shall bar your way."

49

Meanwhile, the Cid, who girt the sword in a blessed hour, had encamped at El Poyo, which will be called in history El Poyo del Cid as long as the Moor and Christian races exist. While there, he raided far and wide, subjecting to tribute the entire valley of the river Martín.

News of his depredations reached Zaragoza, where the Moors were highly angered and alarmed.

The Cid had been at El Poyo for fifteen weeks, and when it became apparent that Minaya was long overdue, the accomplished leader led his entire force from El Poyo at night, leaving his camp deserted. He marched beyond Teruel and came to a halt in the pine grove of Tévar. He devastated the land of this area and forced the city of Zaragoza to pay him tribute.

After the Cid had spent three weeks in this way, Minaya returned from Castile bringing a force of two hundred sword-

girt knights and a vast number of foot soldiers. When the Cid
caught sight of Minaya he galloped out to embrace him, kiss-
ing him on the lips and eyes. Minaya gave him a full report,
keeping nothing back. The Campeador, with a smile of satis-
faction, cried, "Thanks be to God and his holy grace! As long
as life remains to you, Minaya, my own affairs will prosper."

50

O Lord, how greatly did the entire army rejoice at the re-
turn of Minaya Álvar Fáñez, for he had brought greetings
from their cousins and brothers and word of comrades they
had left behind!

51

O Lord, how great was the joy of the Cid, he of the hand-
some beard! For Álvar Fáñez had delivered the money for a
thousand masses and had brought the Cid greetings from his
wife and his daughters. O Lord, how great was his happiness,
nor did he fail to make known his joy.

"Long life to you, Álvar Fáñez! Your worth is more than
ours! A mission well accomplished!"

52

Without delay the Cid, born in an hour of fate, set out on
a night raid with two hundred chosen knights. They left the
fields of Alcañiz devastated and plundered the country round
about. On the third day they returned to their camp.

53

Word of the Cid's raids spread throughout the area. The
inhabitants of Monzón and Huesca were worried in the ex-
treme, but not the people of Zaragoza, who feared no harm

from the Cid Ruy Díaz since they were already paying tribute
to him.

54

They returned to their camp on El Poyo; the Cid, Álvar
Fáñez, and all the rest were elated by the gains their raids had
netted them. The mighty Cid could not keep from smiling as
he addressed his men:

"Hear me, O knights, and I shall tell you the facts. Whoever
remains too long in one place is likely to exhaust his resources.
Tomorrow morning let us ride. We shall abandon this camp
and move on."

And so the Cid pushed on to the pass of Olocau, raiding for
ten days from there to Huesca and to Montalbán. Everywhere
were heard reports of the havoc wrought by the exile from
Castile.

55

Eventually these widespread reports reached the Count of
Barcelona. When the Count learned that his own territory
was being overrun by the Cid, he was moved to anger at the
outrage.

56

The Count, a swaggering scoundrel, blustered, "That Cid
de Vivar is doing me an intolerable wrong, just as once be-
fore he offended me in my own palace when he wounded a
nephew of mine and failed to make amends. Now he is
plundering lands which are under my protection. For his
other offense I did not challenge him nor withdraw my
friendship. But for this new provocation I shall demand
satisfaction."

The Count had great military resources at his command,
and speedily he began to gather them. Great numbers of
Moors and Christians joined him and they set out in pursuit

of the good Cid Ruy Díaz de Vivar. Three days and three nights they traveled, catching up to the Cid in the pine grove of Tévar. So great were their numbers that they were confident of taking him prisoner.

The Cid Don Rodrigo, with the store of riches he had won, had descended a hill and was down in a valley when a message from the Count reached him. Having heard it, the Cid sent back a message of his own, advising the Count to be calm and not to try blocking his way, for the Cid had taken nothing that belonged to him.

Replied the Count, "Not so! Satisfaction shall be mine, not only for the affront of old, but for the present one as well. This Castilian exile will learn what sort of man he has insulted."

Upon the immediate receipt of this reply, the Cid de Vivar realized that the difficulty could not be resolved without a battle.

57

"Ho, my knights! Stow away the booty we have gained; don your armor at once and take up arms. The Count Don Ramón will give us a mighty battle, for his forces of Moors and Christians are almost countless, and he will never give us peace without combat. If we go on, they will continue to pursue us, so let the battle take place on this spot. Draw tight the cinches of the saddles and put on your armor. Down the slope of the hill they come, dressed in elegant breeches. Their cantles give them no support against the thrust of our lances and their cinches hang loose. But we have good Galician saddles,[18] and strong leather protects our legs. A hundred of our knights ought to be enough to overwhelm their hordes. Before they reach the bottom of the hill, let us meet them with our lances, and for every blow you strike, three saddles

[18] The Galician saddles used by the Castilian knights had high, strong backs which helped keep the warrior from being knocked from his mount when he received the blow of his adversary's lance. The Catalans, on the other hand, appear to have used ordinary riding saddles with low cantles.

will be emptied. Today, in this pine grove of Tévar, the Count Don Ramón Berenguer is going to learn the measure of the man whom he comes pursuing to strip of the spoils of battle."

58

By the time the Cid finished speaking, the knights had completed their preparations and were armed and mounted. They espied the forces of the Catalans charging down the slope of the hill, and when they were almost to the bottom and the valley floor, the Cid, born in a blessed hour, ordered the attack. Eagerly and boldly his men obeyed the command, wielding skillfully their pennant-bearing lances, wounding some of the enemy and knocking others from their mounts. He who was born in a blessed hour had won the battle! Not only did he capture Count Don Ramón, but he also won the sword Colada, worth more than a thousand marks.

59

Through this victory the Cid had brought honor to his manly beard.

The captive count was taken to the Cid's tent, where a guard of the Cid's men was placed over him. Leaving the tent, the Cid saw, to his great satisfaction, that as his men assembled they brought booty with them in vast amounts. A mighty feast was prepared for the leader, but Count Don Ramón scorned everything. Food was brought and set before him, yet he refused to eat and taunted his captors. "I would not eat a bite," he affirmed, "for all the gold in Spain. Rather would I lose both body and soul. O, the disgrace of having to yield to such barbarously clad knaves!"

60

"Eat, my Count," said the Cid Ruy Díaz; "eat this bread, and drink some of this wine. If you do as I say, you may go free; if you refuse, you shall never again set eyes on the Christian world as long as you live."

61

"Eat, Don Rodrigo," replied the Count, "and appease your hunger. As for me, I choose to eat nothing and give myself up to death."

By the third day he had not yielded. The Castilians, who were still busy with the division of the great plunder, could not get him to eat a single bite of bread.

62

"Eat something, Count," said the Cid; "for if you do not, you will never see another Christian soul. But if you satisfy my demands and eat, I shall set you free and release two of your noblemen as well."

When the Count heard this offer, his spirits rose. "If you fulfill this promise you have made, O Cid, I shall marvel at the deed all my life."

"Eat, then, my Count; and when you have satisfied your hunger I shall set you free, and two others along with you. But let it be well understood that I do not intend to return one wretched cent of all the booty I have won and you have lost on the field of battle. For great are my needs for those who share my hardship, and we shall continue meeting these needs by taking from you and from others. This shall be our way of life as long as God wills; such must be the life of one whom the King's displeasure has driven from his native land."

Happily, the Count asked for water so that he might wash his hands. It was soon set before him, and the Count, along with the two knights to whom the Cid had offered freedom, began to eat. O Lord, what marvelous appetites!

The Cid, born in a blessed hour, sat down beside the Count. "If you do not eat to my entire satisfaction, we shall stay right here, and the two of us will never part."

Thereupon cried the Count, "Gladly, most gladly." He and his knights fell to with gusto. The Cid, who kept his eye fastened on the performance, was well satisfied, for the Count fairly made his hands fly.

"If it is your pleasure, O Cid, we are ready to leave. Have horses brought for us, and we shall mount at once. Never, since the day I became a count, have I eaten with greater will, nor shall I ever forget the pleasure this meal has given me."

Three palfreys were led out for them, richly saddled. Costly garments were also given to them, cloaks of fur, and mantles. Count Don Ramón took his place between his two knights, and Don Rodrigo the Castilian accompanied them as far as the edge of the camp.

"Now, O Count, be on your way, Frank and free.[19] My thanks to you for the riches you leave in my hands. If you should ever decide to come seeking me with hope of vengeance, just let me know beforehand, and either you will give up further prizes to me or you will take them from me."

"Fear not, O Cid; there is no danger of that. You have taken enough from me to last for a whole year, and I will not even consider seeking battle with you again."

63

The Count rode away in great haste. He kept turning around to look back, for he was afraid the Cid might change his mind and withdraw his promise of freedom, a treachery which the noble Castilian would never commit for all the wealth of the world, for never in his life had he broken his word.

When the Count was gone, the Cid de Vivar turned back to rejoin his men. Greatly did he rejoice when he saw the quality and amount of the booty they had taken. His men had become so rich that they could scarcely know the extent of the wealth they possessed.

[19] In the Spanish, there is a play on the double meaning of the word *franco;* the Cid has set "free" the Count of Barcelona, who is a "Frank."

THE MARRIAGE OF THE CID'S DAUGHTERS

64

Herewith begins anew the story of the deeds of the Cid de Vivar.

After withdrawing from the vicinity of Zaragoza, and from Huesca and Montalbán, the Cid occupied the pass of Olocau. Then he undertook a campaign against the coastal regions, and, turning his march in the direction of the rising sun, he won Jérica, Onda, and Almenara and conquered the area around Burriana.

65

With the help of the Lord God on high, the Cid captured Murviedro; thus, it was clear that he enjoyed the favor of heaven. In the city of Valencia there was more than a little concern.

66

The people of Valencia viewed the Cid's proximity with displeasure and alarm, and in council decided to besiege him. Marching from evening until dawn, they reached Murviedro and set up their camp nearby.

The Cid beheld it in wonder. "Thanks be to God, our Spiritual Father!" he cried. "We are trespassers in this land of theirs, and our presence costs them dearly. We drink their wine and eat their bread. So, they have just cause for coming here to besiege us. This affair will be settled only through battle. Send out the call to those who are bound by pact to aid us: to Jérica, to Olocau, and on to Onda and Almenara; summon, too, the men of Burriana. We shall take to the field

of battle, and I trust in God that our fortunes will not suffer
thereby."

By the third day his allies had gathered, and the Cid, born
in a blessed hour, spoke to them, "Hear me, O men, and may
God save you! Since we left the land of spotless Christianity
—not of our own will, for we had no choice—our fortunes have
ever prospered, give thanks to God. Now, the Moors of
Valencia lie in siege around us. If we hope to stay in these
lands, we must make an example of them.

67

"Let us wait through the night; by dawn let every man
have horse and arms in readiness, and we shall attack their
hosts. Exiles in an alien land are we; soon each of you will
have a chance to prove his worth."

68

Minaya Álvar Fáñez spoke as follows: "O Campeador, may
our deeds ever win your approval. Give me one hundred
knights—I ask for no more. You, with the rest, will make a
frontal attack, bold and strong, while I, with my hundred
men, charge the enemy from the rear, and I trust to God the
battle will be ours."

The plan recommended by Minaya was readily accepted
by the Cid.

Before daylight the men were donning their armor; each
one knew exactly what he was expected to do.

At dawn the Cid attacked, shouting his battle cry: "For
God and the Apostle Saint James! Attack, my men, with fiery
spirit! I am Ruy Díaz! I am the Cid de Vivar!"

In the Moorish camp, tent ropes snapped, stakes gave way,
and tent poles toppled to the ground. But the Moors, by
virtue of their very number, began to rally.

Then from the rear came the attack led by Álvar Fáñez,
and the Moors were forced to yield ground and flee, although

they did so reluctantly. The speed of their horses succeeded in carrying some of them to safety. Two emirs were killed in pursuit, which the Cid's knights pressed clear to Valencia itself.

Having stripped the Moorish camp of the great quantity of plunder it contained, they rode back with it to Murviedro. There a tide of rejoicing swept through the town.

Their next accomplishment was the subjugation of Cebolla and all the lands nearby.

The people of Valencia were distraught with fear, for far and wide was spread the report of the Cid's conquests.

69

His fame continued to spread, even to the lands across the sea. The Cid and his men rejoiced in the favor of God, through whose help they had won such great victories. Raiding parties were sent out at night which made their way to Cullera and Játiva and even as far south as the town of Denia, harassing the lands of the Moors all along the coast. Among their prizes was the fortress of Peña Cadiella with all the estates surrounding it.

70

With Peña Cadiella in the Cid's possession, the distress of the people in Játiva and Cullera mounted; in Valencia the alarm knew no bounds.

71

The Cid spent three years in Moorish territory, sleeping by day, raiding by night, winning one town after another.

72

The people of Valencia lived in such fear that they dared not leave the city, nor did they dare come out to meet the Cid in battle. He inflicted great devastation upon them by ravaging their irrigated gardens and destroying their crops every year. The desperate Valencians could only bewail their fate; nowhere were they able to get food. The father could lend no help to his son, nor the son to his father; friends were unable to lessen each other's suffering.

A great sorrow it is to have no bread, to see women and children die of hunger!

Since they themselves could find no way to remedy their plight, they asked for the King of Morocco's help; he, however, being engaged in war on a large scale with the King of Montes Claros,[1] neither sent them any encouragement nor came to their aid.

This development gladdened the Cid. He set out from Murviedro, traveling during the night, and reached the lands of Monreal by morning. Throughout Aragón and Navarre he sent the call, and to the land of Castile he sent this notice: "Whoever desires to be freed from poverty and to gain great riches, let him come to join the Cid, who plans to ride to war and lay siege to Valencia so that the city may be returned into Christian hands.

73

"Three days shall I wait in Cella del Canal for those who would come with me to besiege Valencia. Let every man come of his own will, and let none come against it."

74

This was the call sent out by the Cid, steadfast champion of battle.

Then he returned to Murviedro, which was already in his possession. The call went out far and wide, and vast numbers from Christian lands, spurred on by the desire for riches,

[1] The term "Montes Claros" designated an area south of the Atlas Mountains in northern Africa.

hastened to join the Cid, whose fame kept spreading throughout the land. While his forces were swelled by new arrivals, not a man deserted the Cid; his resources grew continually greater.

He was gratified to see the size of the force that had gathered, and he decided to delay no longer. He marched on Valencia and attacked; he laid close siege to the city, encircling it so completely that no one was able to enter or leave. He gave the beleaguered inhabitants a certain period of time to see if they could get help from their allies outside the city.[2] Nine whole months passed, and early in the tenth month of the siege the city was forced to capitulate.[3]

Wild was the exultation in the ranks of the Cid on the day Valencia fell to him and he entered the city. Those who before had gone unmounted now rode horses. The amount of gold and silver they won was almost incalculable. All had become rich. The fifth part of the spoils which was the leader's share amounted to thirty thousand marks and countless other treasures.

Great was the joy of the Cid and his followers when his banner was seen flying from the highest tower of the citadel.

75

While the Cid and his men were enjoying a respite from battle, the King of Seville learned of the loss of his tributary at Valencia. He marched against the city with thirty thousand men-at-arms. The battle was joined near the Garden of Valencia, and the handsomely bearded Cid routed the enemy and pursued them into Játiva. The ranks of the Moors were in complete confusion as they crossed the river Júcar; there they drank much more water than they liked as they struggled in the current. The King of Seville was wounded three times before making his escape.

[2] This sporting practice is infrequent in modern warfare!
[3] Valencia fell to the Cid on June 15, 1094.

The Cid returned to Valencia with the plunder from the battle. Although the capture of the city of Valencia had netted him enormous wealth, the booty from this latest victory was greater still. Even to soldiers of the lower ranks fell shares of a hundred silver marks each. The fortunes of the Cid had soared to new heights.

76

Great was the rejoicing of those Christian knights in the companies of the Cid Ruy Díaz, born in a blessed hour.

The Cid's beard kept growing and was quite long by now, for he had sworn in the name of King Alfonso who had exiled him that never would scissors touch his beard, nor a single hair be removed from it until it should call forth the remarks of all, Moors and Christians alike.[4]

And so, the Cid Don Rodrigo took his leisure in Valencia, Minaya Álvar Fáñez ever at his side. Great wealth was bestowed upon all those who had accompanied the illustrious Campeador into exile; the Cid had shown his generosity and earned their gratitude through gifts of houses and other property in Valencia. Those who had joined him later were also well rewarded. The Cid realized that some of the latter might choose to return home, if possible, with the wealth they had acquired. On Minaya's advice, he proclaimed that any man made richer fighting by his side who should depart without dissolving the bonds of vassalage by properly taking leave of the Cid and kissing his hand should be run down and seized, deprived of his booty, and sent to the gallows. Measures were taken to ensure the strict enforcement of this order.

The Cid continued his deliberations with Minaya.

"If it seems wise to you, Minaya, I should like to have a list of those who have joined me of late; what they have won in our battles is to be tallied and recorded. Then, if any should

[4] The long, untrimmed beard was a manifestation of the anguish the Cid felt from having to live as an exile from Castile, and he meant to make known to the world the extent of his grief.

try to desert and his absence should be noted, he shall forfeit his share to those old vassals of mine who are standing guard outside the walls of Valencia."

"Wise indeed," agreed Minaya at once.

77

Ordered to assemble, all his men came to the Cid's palace; once there, a count of their number was made. The Cid had three thousand six hundred men, a figure which warmed his heart and brought a smile to his face.

"Thanks be to God, Minaya, and thanks be to Saint Mary the Mother! When we left Vivar, our force was much smaller. Now we have won much treasure, and more will be ours in days to come.

"If you are willing, Minaya, and if it will not be a hardship, I should like to send you to Castile, where our estates are, to see King Alfonso, my rightful sovereign. I desire to send him a present of one hundred of the horses captured here in battle. Go, take them to him, kiss his hands for me, and entreat him to find in his heart the grace to let me bring my wife Doña Jimena and my daughters from Castile. Then I shall send for them, and this will be the message: 'The Cid's wife and her young daughters are to be allowed to make their way with honor and respect to these alien lands which the Cid and his knights have succeeded in conquering.' "

Then in reply spoke Minaya, "Gladly will I go."

Their talk finished, they began preparations for the trip. The Cid detailed one hundred men to serve Álvar Fáñez as faithful escort on the trip; he also told his knight to take a thousand silver marks to the monastery of San Pedro and give five hundred to Abbot Don Sancho.

78

While they were cheerfully attending to these matters, there arrived from the east an ecclesiastic, Bishop Don Jerónimo by name.[5] A wise and learned man, he was also a formidable warrior, either on foot or in the saddle. He came seeking news of further victories on the part of the Cid, eager for battle against the Moors and declaring that there would be no sorrow ever in Christian hearts if only he could fight and slay enough Moors to satisfy his appetite.

The Cid was delighted upon hearing these words. "Hear me, O Minaya Álvar Fáñez! Since God on high has favored us, let us be properly grateful. I shall make the region of Valencia a diocese and place this good Christian in charge of it. You, Minaya, will take the news of this event to Castile."

79

Don Rodrigo's suggestion met with the high approval of Álvar Fáñez, and Don Jerónimo was made Bishop of Valencia and richly endowed. It gladdened every Christian heart to have a bishop in the area of Valencia. Well content, too, was Minaya as he made his farewell and set out on his journey.

80

Minaya Álvar Fáñez departed for Castile, leaving behind him the lands of Valencia in a state of peace. The names of the places where he stopped along the road are of slight interest and will not be mentioned. Inquiring where he might find Alfonso, he learned that the King had not long before gone to Sahagún but had returned to Carrión;[6] there he could be found. Cheered to learn the whereabouts of the

[5] Don Jerónimo, of the Cluniac order, was summoned to Spain by the Archbishop Bernardo of Toledo from Périgord in the central part of France. Of course he was not a bishop when in 1097 he joined the Cid in Valencia. The Cid, on his own authority, appointed him bishop (an action later sanctioned by the Pope and the previously mentioned archbishop). The scholar-cleric-warrior is a common type in the Middle Ages.

[6] A city in the kingdom of León, from which came, according to legend, the first husbands of the Cid's daughters.

King, Minaya Álvar Fáñez, with the gift of a hundred chargers, took the road to Carrión.

81

King Alfonso had just left mass when Minaya Álvar Fáñez approached him, appropriately dressed in courtly robes. Before the eyes of everyone he knelt at the feet of King Alfonso; suppliantly he kissed his hands and addressed him eloquently:

82

"A favor I beg of you, O King Alfonso, in the name of the Creator! That mighty warrior the Cid beseeches you, his noble sovereign, to grant him the same favor he prays heaven to bestow upon you. He fell from your grace and was ordered into exile, and although in alien lands, he has prospered in great degree. He has taken Jérica and the town called Onda; he has won Almenara and splendid Murviedro, as well as Cebolla, Castejón, and the fortress of Peña Cadiella. In addition, he is now lord of Valencia, where he has established an episcopate. There also the noble Campeador has taken the field five times and won as many victories. God has granted him enormous booty. Here is proof of the claims I make: one hundred chargers, strong and swift, all equipped with saddles and bridles. The Cid, who swears himself your vassal and holds you to be his lord, begs you to receive them as a gift."

The King raised his right hand and made the sign of the cross. "Bless me, Saint Isidore! I hail the wealth the Campeador has won, and his mighty deeds bring pleasure to my heart. I accept the gift of these horses which he sends me."

Although the King was pleased, García Ordóñez [7] was extremely vexed. "It would appear from the way the Cid Campeador does just as he pleases," he complained, "that there is not a single warrior left alive in the land of the Moors."

[7] This petulant fellow is the one whose beard the Cid had tweaked after the defeat of the King of Granada at the beginning of our narrative.

"It is not for you to say," the King told the Count. "In any case, he does me greater service than you do."

Then the noble Minaya continued, "The Cid asks permission, if your heart is inclined to grant it, for his wife Doña Jimena and their two daughters to leave the monastery to which the good Campeador took them, so that they may go to join him in Valencia."

At once the King replied, "Such is my pleasure. The needs of their journey shall be provided while they are traveling within my domain, and I will see that they suffer neither harm nor affront nor dishonor. When the ladies pass beyond my borders, their safekeeping will be in the Cid's hands and yours.

"Hear me now, my vassals, and all those of this my court! I do not want the Cid to suffer any loss. To all those who call themselves vassals of the Cid and hold him to be their lord do I hereby return their confiscated estates; let them retain possession of them, wherever they may go in the service of the Campeador. Further, I charge that no man do them personal harm nor violence. I make this decree in order that the Cid's men may be free to serve their lord."

Minaya Álvar Fáñez kissed the hands of the King, who then smiled and spoke with royal dignity: "Whosoever of you may choose to enter the service of the Campeador are free to go, and may the grace of God go with you. This course of action will profit us more than would continued ill feeling toward the Cid."

At this point the brothers called the Infantes [8] de Carrión began a discussion with each other. "The Cid's renown grows steadily. We could enrich ourselves immensely through marriage with his daughters. But we dare not be the ones to suggest such a marriage because of the difference of family stations, for the Cid is from Vivar, while our family is that of

[8] *Infante* is a term applied variously to the sons of kings and to the sons of certain others of noble birth. The three Infantes de Carrión who figure in *The Cid*—Diego, Fernando, and Asur—were, historically, the sons of Gonzalo Ansúrez and the nephews of Pedro Ansúrez, Count of Carrión. Diego and Fernando, according to the poem, married the Cid's daughters.

the Counts of Carrión." So they said not a word to anyone, and there the matter stood.

Minaya Álvar Fáñez asked his good King's leave to depart. Spoke the King, "And so you go, Minaya? May heaven's grace go with you. I shall send along an official of my court, who, I believe, will be of service on the way. If you take the ladies with you, they will be attended with diligence, and their every need supplied until they reach the border at Medinaceli; from that point on their care will be the Cid's responsibility."

Minaya made his farewell and left the court.

83

The Infantes de Carrión, having come to a decision, joined Minaya on the road and said to him, "Minaya, you are ever a worthy friend; be a friend to us in a certain matter. Bear our greetings to the Cid de Vivar and tell him that we favor his interests in every possible way, and that he will surely lose nothing if he accepts our friendship."

Minaya replied that he had no objection. He rode on, and the Infantes turned back. The former went straightway to San Pedro de Cardeña, where the ladies were staying. How great was their joy when they saw him approaching! Minaya dismounted, and after offering a prayer to Saint Peter, he sought out the ladies. Bowing, he spoke, "Greetings, Doña Jimena, and may God save you and both your little daughters from harm. The Cid sends you greetings from Valencia, where he was well and prosperous when I left him. I have gained the gracious permission of the King to take you to Valencia, which is now in our hands. If only the Cid may see you arrive safely and without harm, he will know unbounded joy, nor any sorrow."

"So be the will of God," said Doña Jimena.

Minaya Álvar Fáñez ordered three knights to ride ahead to the Cid in Valencia. "Tell the Cid—may God keep him from harm—that the King has released his wife and daughters into my charge and has arranged for the needs of the journey

through his territory. In fifteen days, with God's protection, I
shall arrive with his wife and daughters and the good ladies
who serve them."

The knights rode off to fulfill their mission, and Minaya
Álvar Fáñez remained behind in San Pedro.

From everywhere knights came to ask Álvar Fáñez to help
them realize their hopes of joining the Cid in Valencia.

"Gladly will I do so," Minaya told them.

Sixty-five knights had joined him, and counting the hundred
he had brought with him from Valencia, there would be a
strong force to serve as an escort for the ladies.

Minaya gave the Abbot the five hundred marks. Then with
the other five hundred the good Minaya set out to buy for
Doña Jimena, her daughters, and the ladies in waiting, the
most splendid dresses and finery to be had in Burgos; he also
obtained palfreys and mules, so that a good impression would
be made.

The ladies having been suitably attired, Minaya was pre-
paring to mount his horse, when suddenly Raquel and Vidas
fell at his feet and cried, "Take pity on us, Minaya, O illus-
trious knight! Unless the Cid takes care of us, we are ruined.
If he will only repay the amount we lent him, we shall forego
any interest."

"I shall speak to the Cid about it when, God willing, I re-
turn to Valencia, and I promise that you will be richly repaid
for what you have done."

"May God so grant," cried Raquel and Vidas, "for other-
wise, we intend to leave Burgos and go find him."

Back to San Pedro rode Minaya Álvar Fáñez, where even
more men joined his company. As he prepared to mount and
take leave of the Abbot, the moment of farewell filled their
hearts with sorrow.

"God avail you, Minaya Álvar Fáñez! Kiss the hands of the
Campeador for me, and beg him not to forget this monastery
of ours, for his beneficence toward us will forever do him
honor."

Minaya replied that he would be glad to do as bidden.

And so the company said goodby and rode away. Attended by the officer of King Alfonso, they were abundantly provided for on their journey through Castile. Five days out of San Pedro the ladies and Álvar Fáñez reached Medinaceli.

When the Cid received the message delivered by the three knights, his heart overflowed with joy, and from his lips came these words: "From a good messenger may be expected only good messages. You, Muño Gustioz, and you also, Pedro Bermúdez, and Martín Antolínez, worthy man of Burgos, and Bishop Don Jerónimo, eminent cleric, ride at once, and take a hundred horsemen with you, well armed for combat. Take the road through Santa María de Albarracín and on beyond to Molina, the lord of which is Abengalbón, allied to me in peace and friendship. He will join you with another hundred men-at-arms. Proceed straightway to Medinaceli; there I have been told you will find my wife and daughters, escorted by Minaya Álvar Fáñez. Bring them here to me with all due honor. I shall remain in Valencia; its capture cost a fearsome price, and to leave it unprotected would be folly. I shall stay in Valencia, where I am lord and master."

When the Cid finished speaking, the troop rode off, stopping as seldom as possible. They passed through Santa María and spent the night at Bronchales; the next day's journey brought them to Molina, where the Moor Abengalbón came out to receive them with a warm welcome as soon as he learned of their coming.

"Welcome, O vassals of my esteemed friend! I assure you that I feel no sorrow at your arrival—nothing but pleasure."

Muño Gustioz made prompt reply, "The Cid sends you greetings! And he wishes you to furnish us at once a force of a hundred knights. The Cid's wife and daughters are in Medinaceli. He asks that you go with us to get them and bring them here, and that you do not leave their side until we get back to Valencia."

Abengalbón declared that he would be most happy to do so.

That evening Abengalbón had a great repast set before his guests, and the next morning they all rode off together.

Although the Cid had asked him for an escort of one hundred men, Abengalbón brought along two hundred. They passed through a large area of densely wooded country and boldly on through the brush-covered Plain of Taranz, then down through the Arbujuelo Valley.

At Medinaceli, where a constant watch was being kept, Minaya Álvar Fáñez spied an approaching band of armed men. Somewhat concerned, he sent out two riders to discover who they were. Promptly and willingly his orders were carried out. One of his two riders remained there with the band, and the other rode back to report to Álvar Fáñez. "It is a company of the Cid's men who have come to meet us, led by those staunch friends of yours, Pedro Bermúdez and Muño Gustioz; with them are Martín Antolínez of Burgos and that steadfast cleric, Bishop Don Jerónimo. Abengalbón, Moorish lord of Molina, has added his men to the force because he is a friend of the Cid and wishes in this way to do him honor. They are all riding in one company and soon will be here."

"Let us ride!" commanded Minaya, and without delay they did so. What a splendid picture it was! One hundred knights rode out on fine horses caparisoned in silk trappings, bells on their harnesses. The knights carried their shields slung at their necks and bore their lances high with pennants streaming. With this display Álvar Fáñez wished to show the others how diligently and ceremoniously he had escorted the ladies from Castile.

The advance detachment now returned; the knights raised lances and began to disport in games of arms. Gaily they made their way along the river Jalón. When the company from Valencia rode up, they knelt in homage before Minaya. Then Abengalbón arrived, and, as soon as he saw Minaya, smiled and went to embrace him, kissing him on the shoulder in accordance with the custom of his race.

"O happy day, Minaya Álvar Fáñez!" he cried. "You have safely conducted these ladies, by whose presence we are honored, the wife and daughters of the mighty Cid. All respect shall be yours, for such is the fortune of the Cid that, even if we should wish to do so, we could do him no ill. Whatever we have is his, in peace or in war, and a fool is he who does not believe it so."

84

Minaya Álvar Fáñez smiled and replied, "Hail, Abengalbón, the Cid's true friend! If God grants me to return to the Cid and find him alive, I promise that what you have done for him will not go unrewarded. And now let us go to our lodging, for the feast is spread."

"I thank you for your hospitality," said Abengalbón. "Within three days I shall repay it twofold."

They entered Medinaceli, where they all were pleased with the provisions Minaya had made for their comfort. The King's officer took care of the cost of everything. The accommodations afforded the Cid's people there in Medinaceli did honor to the lord of Valencia. There was no expense to Minaya; the King paid for everything.

Night passed, and they set out from Medinaceli the next morning after hearing mass. Over the river Jalón they rode, swiftly up the Valley of Arbujuelo, and in a short time across the Plain of Taranz, and at length to Molina, the city held by Abengalbón.

Day and night the Bishop Don Jerónimo attended the ladies closely, riding a palfrey, and, leading on his right the war horse which bore his arms, Álvar Fáñez rode close by.

When the travelers reached Molina, a wealthy and beautiful city, the Moor Abengalbón provided lavishly; there was no lack of anything they wished. He even had some of their mounts shod at his own expense. He paid Minaya and the ladies the most respectful attention.

Early the next morning they continued their journey. The Moor escorted them faithfully to within sight of Valencia, declining their offers to reimburse him for the cost of the service he had done them. Amidst expressions of joy at the successful outcome of events, they came to within three leagues of Valencia. At that point word of their arrival was sent ahead to the one who had girt the sword in a blessed hour.

85

Nothing had ever gladdened the Cid's heart more than this good news of the ones he loved most in the world. At once he sent out two hundred knights to meet Minaya and the noble ladies. He himself stayed in Valencia to guard the city, for he well knew that Álvar Fáñez had taken every necessary precaution.

86

The band of knights received Minaya, Doña Jimena, her daughters and ladies, and the rest of the company.

The Cid ordered his men to set a guard over the citadel, the other lofty towers, and at every one of the city's entrances and exits. Then he had them bring him Babieca, a charger he had won from the King of Seville in his recent victory. The Cid, who girt the sword in a blessed hour, had as yet no idea how fast or well-trained the steed would be. He wanted to perform the ceremonial practice of knightly arms for his wife and daughters while not too far from the safety of Valencia's walls.

The ladies were welcomed with great honor. Bishop Don Jerónimo rode on ahead of the company to the city; he dismounted in front of the chapel and entered. Having formed a procession of the greatest possible number of clerics, clad in surplices and bearing silver crosses, the Bishop moved out to receive the ladies and the good knight Minaya.

The Cid, born in a blessed hour, swiftly donned his tunic; his beard flowed long and free. Saddle and trappings were placed on Babieca. Out rode the Cid, bearing wooden lance and shield. On his charger, Babieca, he made an extraordinary run, so swift that all who saw it marveled. From that day on, Babieca's worth became known throughout all Spain.

After he had raced his charger, the Cid dismounted and hurried toward his wife and two daughters. As he approached, Doña Jimena threw herself at his feet, crying:

"Hail, Campeador! God bless the day you girt the sword! You have delivered me from woeful hardship. Behold, by God's grace and your efforts, here am I, and here are your daughters, genteel and good."

Then he embraced the mother and her girls, and tears welled up in their eyes from the joy they felt. The knights of his company shared in the jubilation, engaging in sportive games of arms, jousting and tilting at wooden scaffolds.

Then spoke the Cid, who girt the sword in a blessed hour, "Doña Jimena, beloved and honored wife, and my daughters, my very heart and soul, come with me into the city of Valencia, into this estate which I have won for you."

Mother and daughters kissed his hands and in due honor entered Valencia.

87

The Cid led the ladies to the citadel and took them up to its very top. From there, they cast the gaze of their beautiful eyes in every direction over the city of Valencia spread below them. On one side lay the sea; they viewed the broad, luxuriant, irrigated fields called the Garden, and many other marvels. They lifted their hands to thank God for this good and bountiful prize.

Life there was pleasant for the Cid and his people. Winter was over, and March was drawing near.

Now you shall hear of King Yúsuf of Morocco and of events taking place in that land across the sea.

88

This Moroccan king was burning with anger toward the Cid Don Rodrigo. "He has savagely invaded territory which belongs to me," he complained. "And he gives thanks for his success to nobody but Jesus Christ!" He then began to mobilize his strength, and with a mighty force of fifty thousand men-at-arms on board his ships he set sail for Valencia to attack the Cid Don Rodrigo. The vessels landed, and the men disembarked.[9]

89

Arriving at Valencia, now in the hands of the Cid, the host of infidels pitched their tents and built their camp. The Cid was informed of this fact.

90

"Thanks be to God our Spiritual Father!" cried the Cid. "All I own lies spread before me. With great difficulty did I take Valencia, which I hold as my estate, and only death shall force me to relinquish it. Thanks to the Creator and to Saint Mary, Mother of God, my wife and daughters are here with me. All these from lands beyond the sea bring only delight to me. I cannot avoid taking the field, and my wife and daughters will watch me do battle; with their own eyes they shall see how we live in this foreign land and how we win our bread."

Then he brought his wife and daughters to the top of the citadel; from there they could see the Moors erecting their tents.

"God save you, what is happening, my Cid?" asked Jimena.

"Have no fear, my honored wife. It is a vast and splendid fortune that has come to make us richer. Scarcely have you arrived when the Moors come bearing you gifts. Your daughters are yet to marry, and the Moors are bringing you their dowry."

"I thank you, my Cid, and thanks be to God on high."

"I want you to remain here in this palace, my wife, in this

---

[9] As a matter of historical fact, Yúsuf himself did not lead this expedition against Valencia, perhaps out of respect for the Cid's fame as a warrior, but sent his cousin as emir of the Moorish forces.

citadel, and do not be afraid when you see me in combat; with the help of God and Holy Mother Mary I shall win this battle, for my heart gathers strength from the fact that you will be watching me."

91

The Moors have finished pitching their tents. As dawn breaks, their drums set up a frenzied beating.

"O what a great day is this!" exults the Cid.

But his wife is filled with heart-bursting terror, as are her ladies and her two daughters; never before in their lives have they heard such a fearful noise.

Stroking his beard, the good Cid Campeador comforted them. "Have no fear, for things will turn out well for you. Within two weeks, God willing, those drums will be our trophies, and I shall have them brought before you for your inspection; then they will be taken to the Bishop Don Jerónimo to be hung in the Cathedral of Santa María, Mother of God."

This is the vow the Cid Campeador makes.

The ladies are reassured, losing their terror little by little.

Riding swiftly, the host from Morocco fearlessly pours into the Garden of Valencia.

92

As soon as the sentinel in Valencia catches sight of them, he rings a bell to sound the alarm. The bands of the Cid Ruy Díaz are ready; after careful attention to their arms, they charge from the city. They close swiftly with the Moors wherever they meet them, routing them from the Garden. On this day a full five hundred Moors meet their deaths.

93

Pressing the pursuit to the very camp of the Moors, the Christians ride back from the battle, having accomplished

much for the day. Álvar Salvadórez has fallen prisoner to the
Moors.[10] The vassals of the Cid return to his side, and al-
though he himself has seen the action, they report to him the
capture of Álvar Salvadórez.

Well content with their performance, the Cid addresses his
men: "Hear me, O knights. So must it be.

"This has been a great day, and tomorrow will be even
greater. Tomorrow let every man be armed before dawn.
Bishop Don Jerónimo will give us absolution and sing mass
for us.[11] Then resolutely we shall ride into battle in the face
of the foe, and on our lips will be the name of the Creator and
the Apostle Saint James. Either we vanquish them or they will
deprive us of bread."

With one voice his men exclaim, "So shall it be!"

Then at once speaks Minaya: "As you wish, O Cid, but give
me a different assignment. Let me have a hundred and thirty
knights for the battle, and while you charge the enemy in the
front, I shall attack from the rear. Then will God favor one
of us or the other, or even both."

The Cid agrees without delay to this plan of action.[12]

94

The day draws to a close, night falls, and the Christians
hasten to make ready their battle gear. Long before daylight
Bishop Don Jerónimo offers mass for them and afterward gen-
eral absolution.

"Whoever may die this day in honorable combat is hereby
absolved of sin, and may God receive his soul.

"My Cid Don Rodrigo, heaven blessed the day you girt the

10 Although the poet neglects to give us the details, Álvar Salvadórez
must have regained his freedom, for he reappears further on in the poem.

11 Before a battle, the Mass of the Holy Trinity was sung and absolu-
tion dispensed for the special benefit of those who might be killed in
"honorable" combat.

12 This is the same maneuver proposed by Álvar Fáñez and employed in
a previous battle near Murviedro.

sword! This morning I have said mass for you, and in return
I ask you for the honor of dealing the first blows of the
battle."

Replied the Campeador, "So be it granted."

95

Out through the gates of Cuarto come the warriors, and
the Cid gives them their final instructions. Knights of known
dependability are left to guard the gates of the city. With a
leap the Cid mounts his charger, Babieca, who is decked out
in all his trappings. Close behind his standard, thirty less
than four thousand of the Cid's knights sally boldly forth
from the city of Valencia and attack the Moorish army of fifty
thousand. Álvar Álvarez and Minaya strike from the rear, and
God grants to the Christians the power to rout the enemy.

First, the Cid wields his lance, then he draws his sword and
slays uncounted Moors; his arm is drenched to the elbow with
their blood. Three times he strikes King Yúsuf but the Moor
escapes the sword at full gallop and seeks safety in the palatial
fortress of Cullera, pursued by the Cid and some of his loyal
vassals. The Cid, born in a blessed hour, then turns back, well
satisfied with the spoils they have captured. Now he knows
Babieca's worth from nose to tail. All the plunder is now in
his hands. A reckoning of the enemy forces discloses that only
a hundred and four of the fifty thousand have escaped. The
Cid's men, while stripping the Moroccan camp, collect three
thousand marks in gold and silver, along with countless other
prizes. The rejoicing of the Cid and his vassals is complete,
for God has availed them, and they have won the battle.

The King of Morocco defeated, the Cid left Álvar Fáñez in
charge of reckoning the booty and entered Valencia with a
hundred knights. He had removed his helmet and hood of
mail, revealing the wrinkled cloth cap above his face. With
sword in hand he rode Babieca into the city. There the ladies,
who had been waiting for him, received him. The Cid reined
his horse to a halt before them.

"I bow before you, my ladies, in whose name I have won great renown. While you have held Valencia, I have prevailed on the field of battle. No sooner have you arrived in Valencia than God and all his saints have granted a vast fortune to come into our hands. See my bloody sword, and see my horse lathered with sweat. These are the tools with which we conquer the Moors in battle! Pray God to grant me more years of life, and honor will be yours, and people will kiss your hands in homage."

Saying this, the Cid dismounted, whereupon his daughters, his noble wife, and the ladies in waiting knelt before him.

"Long life to you, our lord!"

Then they went with him into the palace, where they sat by his side on fine benches.

"My wife Doña Jimena, since you have asked me before to do so, I propose to arrange marriages with some of my vassals for these ladies you have brought here and who serve you so loyally. I shall give each of them a dowry of two hundred marks, and let the people of Castile know the stature of the lady they serve. As for the marriage of your daughters, we must be in no haste."

All the ladies rose to kiss his hand, and joy spread throughout the palace. And indeed, the dowries were presented and the matches made, just as the Cid had promised.

On the battlefield, Minaya Álvar Fáñez and his aides were counting and recording the plunder. They collected an enormous wealth of tents, weapons, and costly raiment. But the richest prizes consisted of the fully equipped war horses. There were so many of them that the exact number could not be determined, as there were not enough men to catch them all. To even the local Moors there fell a sizable share of the booty. And yet, the Cid's portion amounted to a thousand of the finest chargers. While the Cid's lot was so large, the others were well rewarded, too. What magnificent Moorish pavilions, what lavishly carved tent poles, fell prize to the Cid and his vassals! The Cid Campeador gave orders that one of the tents was to be left standing, that nobody was to strike it. This had belonged to the King of Morocco and was the most magnificent of all; it was supported by two poles decorated with wrought gold.

"This is such a splendid Moroccan tent that I am going to send it to Alfonso the Castilian so that he will know how great a treasure I have won."

Then all this rich booty was taken into the city of Valencia. There, that illustrious man of the church, Bishop Don Jerónimo, his thirst for battle slaked by hand-to-hand combat, did not know how many Moors he had slain. His share of the booty was especially abundant, for the Cid Don Rodrigo, born in a blessed hour, made him a present of a tenth of his own part.

96

Great was the rejoicing of the Christians throughout Valencia at the wealth of money, horses, and arms they had won. Great was the joy of Jimena and her daughters, and that of their ladies, whose marriages were now assured.

Without losing a day the good Cid said, "Come here, my loyal knight Minaya. You have well and fairly won the booty which fell to your lot. Now I insist that you take from my share all you wish, and let the rest be mine.

"Tomorrow morning you are to set out with two hundred of the chargers I won as my share, all equipped with saddles and bridles, and a like number of swords. You will present them to King Alfonso, so that he may not speak ill of the lord of Valencia. And let this gift in the name of my wife and daughters express their gratitude to the King for his permission that they might come to me."

He ordered Pedro Bermúdez to accompany Minaya. The next morning they set out in haste with two hundred horsemen in their company; with them they took the gift of two hundred horses won on the field of battle by the Cid, as well as the Cid's greetings and pledge of vassalage to the King and his promise of steadfast service until his soul and body should part.

97

They set out on their journey, leaving Valencia behind them. They knew well the care they must take to guard the treasure in their possession. Day and night they traveled without stopping to rest; they crossed the mountain range which marked the border and began to inquire as to the whereabouts of King Don Alfonso.

98

After crossing mountains, forests, and rivers, they reached Valladolid, where the King was at the time. Pedro Bermúdez and Minaya sent word to the King, asking him to receive this company which was bringing presents from the Cid, lord of Valencia.

99

The King, overjoyed, ordered his noblemen to mount at once, and, with the King himself at their head, they rode swiftly out to learn the object of the Cid's delegation. Among the courtiers were the Infantes de Carrión and the Cid's mortal enemy, the Count Don García. The arrival of the band was welcome to some of the court, but to others it brought some anxiety, for as they drew to within sight of the Cid's men, the latter appeared at first to be a hostile party rather than emissaries. King Don Alfonso kept making the sign of the cross.

Minaya and Pedro Bermúdez rode forward; dismounting and falling to their knees, they kissed the ground and the King's feet.

"Hail, O honored King Alfonso! We kiss your feet in the name of the Cid Campeador, who calls you his lord and holds himself your vassal. Greatly he esteems the favor that has come to him from your hand. Not many days ago, O King, he conquered in battle, defeating the Moroccan King Yúsuf and driving his host of fifty thousand from the field. Great were the prizes taken, and all the Cid's vassals were made rich. Now he sends you this gift of two hundred chargers, and he kisses your hands."

Replied King Alfonso, "I am pleased to accept them, and I thank the Cid for such a gift as this. May the hour come when he may be repaid."

Many approved the King's acceptance and kissed his hands. But Count Don García felt only annoyance; angrily he drew aside with ten of his relatives.

"What a prodigy is that Cid," he scoffed, "whose honors prosper so! The brighter his glory, the dimmer our own. For our prestige will suffer, just because he has conquered a few kings in battle, with little more effort than if he had found them lying dead, and driven off their mounts."

100

King Don Alfonso spoke as follows: "Thanks be to God and to the noble Saint Isidore for these two hundred horses which the Cid has sent me. As long as I am king I shall count on even greater services from him.

"I hereby order that you, Minaya Álvar Fáñez and Pedro Bermúdez, be dressed richly from my largess and provided with whatever arms you desire, so that you may present a proper appearance before the Cid Ruy Díaz. Take these three horses as my gift to you.

"It seems very clear to me, for my heart tells me so, that great things will ensue from all these exploits."

101

The knights kissed his hands and then went to put up for the night. The King's orders were that their every need should be supplied.

Now let us turn back to the Infantes de Carrión, who were secretly fashioning their designs.

"The Cid's affairs grow ever more prosperous. Let us ask his daughters' hands in marriage and thus enhance our honor and our fortune."

And so they went to King Alfonso with their request.

102

"A favor we come to ask of you, O King and lord. If it is your pleasure, we pray you ask the hands of the Cid's daughters for us; we desire to marry them as much to increase their honor as our own fortune."

The King considered for a long time. "I am the one who ordered the Cid into exile, and while I have done a disservice to him, he has labored faithfully in my behalf; I am not sure that the proposed marriages will be to his liking. But since your desire is so, let us undertake the arrangements."

King Don Alfonso had Minaya Álvar Fáñez and Pedro Bermúdez summoned to his presence, and, taking them aside into another room, said to them, "Hear me, Minaya, and you, Pedro Bermúdez! I have decided to offer pardon to the Cid Campeador Ruy Díaz, for he has earned it fully through his services to me. He may come for a meeting with me if he so pleases.

"Another matter has developed here at my court: Diego and Fernando, the Infantes de Carrión, seek the hands of his two daughters in marriage. You will kindly bear this message to the good Campeador and advise him that honor and prestige will accrue to him through union with the family of the Infantes de Carrión."

Then spoke Minaya, whose words bore the approval of Pedro Bermúdez. "We shall convey your request to the Cid, and then let him decide what course he may choose to follow."

"Tell Ruy Díaz, born in a blessed hour, that I am willing

to meet him at some suitable location; the meeting will be held wherever he may decide. It is my desire to promote in all respects the interests of the Cid."

Thereupon the two knights took leave of the King and returned with their company to Valencia. As soon as the Cid learned of their approach, he rode out to meet them and with a smile embraced them warmly.

"And so you are back, Minaya, and you, Pedro Bermúdez! The equals of you two men are rare in any land! What news do you bring of my lord King Alfonso? Did he accept my gift, and was he pleased with it?"

"It pleased his very heart and soul," replied Minaya, "and he sends you expressions of his favor."

"God be praised!" cried the Cid.

Next they told their leader of King Alfonso of León's request that the Cid give his daughters in marriage to the Infantes de Carrión; the King, they declared, strongly urged the match because of the honor and prestige which would accrue from such a family connection.

After the noble Cid Campeador heard their report he remained in deep thought for some time. "Thanks be to Christ my Lord! I was cast into exile, and my estates were taken from me; I have had to toil to win what I now possess. Once more, thank God, I find myself in the King's favor. Furthermore, he asks my daughters' hands for the Infantes de Carrión. Tell me, Minaya, and you, Pedro Bermúdez, what do you think of this marriage?"

"We shall stand by whatever you choose to do."

"The Infantes de Carrión," said the Cid, "are of noble birth and very proud; they hold an important position in the King's court. And yet, I should not approve of this marriage, except that it is urged by one of such exalted rank. Let us discuss it among ourselves, and may God on high direct us to the right decision."

"Another thing," said Minaya; "the King sent word that he would come to meet you at a place of your own choosing, for he wants to see you and formally bestow his favor upon you. At that time you could decide what best to do."

"This pleases me to the depths of my heart," declared the Cid.

"Decide, then, upon the place for this meeting," said Minaya.

"If King Alfonso should so desire, I myself should properly be the one to make my way to his presence, an honor due my King and lord. But since he wishes it otherwise, let his pleasure be ours. Let the audience take place on the mighty river Tajo, and let my lord the King set the day."

The Campeador wrote a message saying that he would do as the King wished; he sealed it, and sent it off by two horsemen.

103

The couriers delivered the letter to the honored King, who received it with pleasure. To them he said, "Bear my greetings to the Cid, who girt the sword in a blessed hour. It is decreed that our conference take place three weeks from this day; I shall be there without fail, if there is life in me."

The messengers returned to the Cid without delay, and both parties began to make preparations for the interview.

Never before in all Castile had there been seen so many priceless mules, fast-pacing palfreys, war horses swift and strong, brilliant pennants flying on sturdy lances, shields embossed with gold and silver, cloaks and furs and fine Andrian silks. The King ordered lavish provisions to be taken to the appointed site of the meeting on the shores of the Tajo. A numerous retinue accompanied him. The Infantes de Carrión, their spirits elated by the thought that all the gold and silver they could wish for would soon increase their fortune, kept borrowing money in one place and spending it in another. King Don Alfonso rode off at a fast pace, accompanied by counts and royal magistrates and numerous vassals. The Infantes de Carrión also had a large following with them. Leonese, Galicians, and a multitude of Castilians swelled the company of the King. With loosened reins they headed for the conference site.

104

In Valencia the Cid Campeador was also making hurried preparations for the interview with the King. Many strong mules, fine palfreys, splendid arms, good, speedy war horses, beautiful capes, mantles, and furs were made ready; men and children alike were arrayed in garments of brilliant hue.

Minaya Álvar Fáñez; Pedro Bermúdez; the lord of Monte Mayor, Martín Muñoz; the illustrious man from Burgos, Martín Antolínez; that noble man of the church, Bishop Don Jerónimo; Álvar Álvarez; Álvar Salvadórez; the excellent knight, Muño Gustioz; and the Aragonese, Galindo García—these and all his other vassals made ready to accompany the Cid Campeador.

The Campeador ordered Álvar Salvadórez and Galindo García of Aragón and all the knights in their command to guard the city of Valencia with the utmost precaution. According to the Cid's instructions, the gates of the citadel were not to be opened day or night; for that was where his wife and daughters, dear to his heart and soul, were staying with their faithful ladies in waiting. The Cid, born in a blessed hour, laid down the most careful instructions that not one of the ladies should leave the citadel until his return.

They rode out of Valencia and set spurs to their palfreys. To the right of him each man led his war horse, swift and strong, chargers which the Cid had won on the field of battle —they had certainly not come to him as a gift. Thus he proceeded toward the site of the conference he had arranged with the King.

When King Alfonso, who had arrived the day before, learned that the good Campeador was approaching, he led a band out to receive him with all respect. As soon as the King came into sight, the Cid, born in a blessed hour, ordered all his men to halt except some fifteen knights who were dearest to his heart; with these he leaped to the ground, just as he had planned to do. Then falling to his hands and knees he took the grass of the field in his teeth, tears of elation streaming from his eyes. In this way did he render obeisance to his lord Alfonso; then he knelt at the King's feet.

King Don Alfonso's heart was touched. "Arise, O Cid Campeador," he ordered; "you may kiss my hands, but if you kiss my feet, you will arouse my displeasure."

The Campeador remained kneeling. "I beg of you your favor, my lord! On bended knees I implore your pardon, and let all men present hear it awarded."

Said the King, "Right willingly I do so. I hereby pardon you and bestow upon you my favor from this day on, and I bid you welcome in all parts of my kingdom."

"I thank you, my lord Alfonso," replied the Cid, "and I accept your pardon, making known my gratitude first to God on high, then to you, and to these men present."

Still kneeling, he kissed the King's hands; then he arose and kissed his lips. All the onlookers rejoiced at the sight— all except Álvar Díaz and García Ordóñez, who bore it bitterly.

"Thanks be to God the Father," the Cid exclaimed, "for I have regained the favor of my lord Alfonso! God will protect me night and day! Now, if you will, my lord, be my guest."

"That would not be right," replied the King, "for you have just arrived, and we have been here since yesterday. You are to be my guest today, Cid Campeador, and tomorrow I shall accept your invitation."

The Cid kissed the King's hand and deferred to his wishes.

Then the Infantes de Carrión came over to pay their respects. "We salute you, O Cid, born in a heaven-blessed hour, and offer you a pledge of our friendship."

"May God so grant," replied the Cid.

The Cid Ruy Díaz, born in a blessed hour, was that day the guest of the King, who paid him constant attention and manifested a great regard for him; he kept eying the Cid's beard, which had grown abundant in such a short time. The Cid, indeed, was the marvel of all eyes.

And so the day was spent, and night came on; the next day dawned bright and clear. The Cid Campeador had his servants prepare a feast for everybody there, and so thoroughly did he discharge his obligations of hospitality that all were glad to agree that they had not eaten better in several years.

As the sun rose the next morning, Bishop Don Jerónimo sang mass. After leaving the church they all assembled, and the King at once began to address them:

"Hear me, O men of my court, counts and nobles! I wish to propose a matter to the Cid Campeador; may Christ grant that it be to his best interest. O Cid, I ask you to give your daughters, Doña Elvira and Doña Sol,[13] in marriage to the Infantes de Carrión. The union is an honorable one and advantageous, as I think; the Infantes seek it, and I endorse it. On one side and on the other, may all here, both your men and mine, support this suit. Give us your daughters, O Cid, and may God reward you therefor."

"The time is not yet at hand for them to marry," responded

[13] Historical evidence establishes the fact that the Cid had two daughters, but documents refer to them as Cristina and María. It seems possible that the baptismal names were used in official documents, while other names or "pet" names were ordinarily used within the family and circle of acquaintances. Thus a girl named Alice Virginia might be called Virginia, or A. V. by her family and friends, but her legal name would be Alice. Furthermore, "eyes," "life," all sorts of flowers and birds (cf. *Amapola, La Paloma*), "heaven" (cf. *Cielito Lindo*), "sun" (cf. *O Sole Mio*), etc., are used in Latin countries as terms of endearment for girls. "Sol" might thus be the name which the poet preferred to use.

No record exists of the marriage of the Cid's daughters to the Infantes de Carrión; it is probably an invention of the poet, one of the few departures in the epic from historicity, and at the same time one of the most important motifs of the epic's structure. The Cid's older daughter Cristina (Elvira) did, in fact, marry the Infante Ramiro de Navarre, as is related at the final part of the epic. But María (Sol) was married to Count Ramón Berenguer III of Barcelona, not to the Infante de Aragón.

the Cid, "for they are of tender age, and their years are few. Yet the Infantes de Carrión are of great renown, suitable husbands for my daughters and even deserving of wives of higher station. I am their father, and yet, since they were reared in your court,[14] their future, as well as mine, is yours to dispose. I give Doña Elvira and Doña Sol over into your hands; marry them to the husbands of your choice, and I shall not complain."

"My thanks to you and to all this court," said the King.

Then the Infantes de Carrión arose and came over to kiss the hands of the one who was born in a blessed hour; they exchanged swords with the Cid in the presence of King Don Alfonso.[15]

Then spoke good King Alfonso in noble tones, "My thanks to you, illustrious Cid, and most of all my thanks to God that you have given me your daughters for the Infantes de Carrión. Herewith, I receive into my hands Doña Elvira and Doña Sol and give them in marriage to the Infantes de Carrión. With your consent I wed them,[16] and may God grant that the marriages bring you joy.

"In your hands I place the Infantes de Carrión; they are to go with you, for I shall be far away. I shall give them three hundred silver marks toward the cost of the wedding celebration,[17] or for whatever you think fit. Once your sons-in-law are under your charge in mighty Valencia, they, as much as

14 Cf. note, p. 30.

15 This ceremony of exchanging swords formalized on the part of both parties the establishment of a family relationship. Later on, the Cid will give the Infantes his two prize swords, Colada and Tizón, when the Infantes leave Valencia for Carrión with their brides. Finally, the Infantes are required to return Colada and Tizón as a token of the dissolution of the family ties. Also, I imagine, the Cid wanted to get them back because of their considerable material worth.

16 What may appear to be a wedding *in absentia* is only the King's formal edict that the marriage is to take place. Elaborate ceremonies will be held later in Valencia.

17 According to the strictly drawn conventions of medieval society, the lord was expected to help defray the cost of celebrating the marriage of a vassal's daughter.

your daughters, will be your children one and all, and you may do as you like with the money."

The Cid received the marks and kissed the King's hands. "Many thanks I give you, my lord and King! It is you who gives my daughters in marriage, not I."

An accord was reached and the decision made that the next day at sunrise the two parties were to return to their respective homes.

Then the Cid Campeador did an extraordinary thing. He began to hand out as gifts to whoever wanted them the strong mules, fine palfreys, and beautiful, costly garments which he had brought with him. Nobody was refused what he asked. The Cid gave away sixty chargers. Everybody who had attended the audience felt pleased with events, and now all were on the point of departing, for night was coming on.

The King took the Infantes by the hand and gave them over to the Cid Campeador. "These are your sons, since they are now your daughters' husbands. From this day on, Campeador, they are yours to command; may they regard you as a father and respect you as their lord."

"I accept what you have given me, O King, and I thank you. May God in heaven grant you the reward you deserve.

105

"I ask of you a favor, my King. Since you have arranged the marriage to suit yourself, name another in my stead to hand over the brides to you, for never with my own hand will I do so and thereby give the Infantes this satisfaction." [18]

"Then let Álvar Fáñez be the one," replied the King. "Take them by the hand and give them to the Infantes, just as I have received them into my own hands from this great distance, as though they were actually standing here in our presence. And you, Álvar Fáñez, will be their sponsor in all the

---

[18] It is clear that the Cid does not like the prospect of his daughters' marriages to the Infantes, but his bonds of vassalage prevent him from objecting to his king's action.

rites of the wedding, and you will give me an account of the affair the next time we meet."

"I shall be pleased to do so," promised Álvar Fáñez.

106

The arrangements were sealed with solemn pledges of fulfillment.

"Now, King Alfonso, my honored lord, accept from me a present to mark this occasion of our meeting: I have brought you thirty palfreys, richly caparisoned, and also thirty swift chargers, each with a fine saddle; they are my gift to you, and I beg you to accept them."

Said King Alfonso, "I am overwhelmed by this gift you offer me. Yet I accept it, and may it please the Creator and all his saints to reward you well for the pleasure it brings me. My Cid Ruy Díaz, you have done me much honor and served me well, and I am well content with you. May I live to repay you some day. Now may God be with you, for I am leaving this meeting. God in heaven grant that each party will fulfill the terms of our accord."

107

The Cid leaped upon his charger Babieca. "Here, in the presence of my lord King Alfonso, I proclaim that whoever desires to attend the wedding ceremonies and receive something from my largess is welcome to come with me, and I do not doubt that he will profit thereby."

Then the Cid took leave of Alfonso, his lord, and rode off, not wishing the King to ride out with him to bid him goodby.

Then many a fortunate knight came up to kiss the King's hands and seek his permission to leave.

"Grant us leave, if it is your pleasure, to go with the Cid's company to Valencia and attend the nuptials of the Infantes de Carrión and the Cid's daughters, Doña Elvira and Doña Sol."

The King gladly gave his permission to all. The Cid's company was increased and the King's retinue diminished, for great numbers chose to go with the Campeador. And so they set out for Valencia, which the Cid had won at the height of his fortune. Two of the best knights in his following, Pedro Bermúdez and Muño Gustioz, were charged with the task of attending the Infantes de Carrión and learning what they could about their dispositions. With Diego and Fernando traveled their brother Asur González, a troublemaker and a great talker, and of little worth in other matters. The greatest respect was shown the Infantes de Carrión.

At length they reached Valencia, where the Cid was master; their spirits soared as they came within sight of the city. The Cid gave the following instructions to Don Pedro and Muño Gustioz: "Take the Infantes de Carrión to their quarters, and stay by their side to attend them. Tomorrow morning at sunrise they will meet their wives, Doña Elvira and Doña Sol."

108

All went to their quarters for the night. The Cid made his way to the citadel, where he was received by Doña Jimena and his daughters.

"Welcome, O Campeador! God bless the hour you girt the sword, and may he grant us long years of life with you!"

"Thanks be to the Creator, I have returned, my honored wife. And I have brought you sons-in-law who will be an honor to our family. You may well be grateful to me, my daughters, for you are wedded well."

109

His wife and daughters, and even their ladies in waiting, kissed the Cid's hands.

"Thanks be to God, and to you, my Cid of the beautiful beard!" cried Doña Jimena. "You have done well, as always. Never so long as you live will our daughters suffer want."

"When you give us in marriage, our fortunes will mount."

110

"Thanks be to God, my wife Doña Jimena. I agree, my daughters Doña Elvira and Doña Sol, that our family will be honored by this marriage. But I want you to understand that the arrangements were not begun by me; my lord Alfonso asked for you so insistently and with such a will that I could not refuse. I placed you in his hands, my daughters, and he, believe me, not I, is the one who gives you in marriage."

111

They set about decorating the palace, covering the floors and walls with cloth of royal purple, with silks and other rich material, making it a rare pleasure to be a guest there.

With all his knights assembled the Cid sent for the Infantes de Carrión, who mounted their horses and shortly appeared at the palace, lavishly accoutered in full chivalric regalia. They dismounted and entered with all decorum and humility. The Cid and his vassals received them, and they in turn bowed before the Cid and his lady, then seated themselves on a costly bench. The Cid's men respectfully gave their attention to the one who was born in a blessed hour.

The Campeador arose. "Let there be no more delay in what must be done. Come, Álvar Fáñez, whom I love and esteem. I give both my daughters into your hands, for I have promised the King to do so, nor will I fail to comply with the pact. Hand them over to the Infantes de Carrión; then let the benediction be pronounced and the matter done."

"Willingly I do so," said Minaya.

The girls stood, and Minaya handed them over to the Infantes de Carrión, to whom he spoke the following words: "I,

Minaya, stand before you, Infantes de Carrión, who are brothers. In the name of King Alfonso and by royal command I give to you these two ladies of noble line; take them for your honored and lawful wives."

With heart and will the Infantes received them, and then went over to kiss the hands of the Cid and Doña Jimena.

This ceremony over, they left the palace and made their way at once to the Cathedral of Santa María; there, Bishop Don Jerónimo, already robed for the occasion, was waiting for them at the entrance to the church. He pronounced the nuptial benediction and then sang mass.

Leaving the church, they mounted without delay and raced to the parade ground near Valencia, where the Cid and his vassals disported in games of knightly arms; he himself changed horses three times. The Cid was highly pleased with what he saw there, for the Infantes de Carrión proved themselves superior horsemen.

They returned to Valencia with the ladies and took part in lavish festivities held in the beautiful citadel. The next day the Cid ordered seven jousting scaffolds erected, all of which the knights leveled before coming in for the noonday feast.

The wedding festival lasted two full weeks, at the end of which the nobles made ready to depart. The Cid Don Rodrigo, born in a blessed hour, made presents to his guests of at least a hundred animals—palfreys, mules, and swift war horses—and gifts of cloaks and furs and many other garments, as well as an untold amount of money. Likewise, his vassals most graciously made presents to those who had attended, giving generously to whoever would accept; those who had come to the wedding went back to Castile much wealthier. The departing guests said farewell to Ruy Díaz, born in a blessed hour, and to the ladies and noblemen of Valencia, and they rode away well content with the Cid and his vassals, praising them highly, as well they might. No less content were Diego and Fernando, the sons of the Count Don Gonzalo.

The guests return to Castile, and the Cid and his sons-in-law remain in Valencia. There the Infantes dwell for nearly

two years, treated with kindness and esteem. Life for the Cid
and his vassals is pleasant.

O, would to the Holy Spirit and Saint Mary that the Cid
and the one who arranged the marriage may never have cause
for regret!

*Thus ends this part of the story. May God and all his saints
watch over you.*

✦✦ III ✦✦

THE ATROCITY IN THE FOREST OF CORPES

112

One day during the time the Cid and his men, including his sons-in-law, the Infantes de Carrión, were living in Valencia, the Cid was lying on a bench asleep. Then an alarming thing happened—the lion undid his leash and broke out of his cage.[1] Terror spread through the hall. The Cid's vassals spread their capes over their arms and formed a screen to protect their lord.

Fernando González, one of the Infantes de Carrión, could find no way to escape, no open room to run into nor any turret to climb. Finally he dived fearfully under the bench [2] on which the Cid was sleeping.

Diego González, his brother, dashed out through a door screaming, "Never again will I see Carrión!" Terrified, he

[1] There was a law concerned with the precautions to be taken by those who kept in their castles wild beasts such as lions, bears, jaguars, leopards, hunting lynxes, and even serpents. Menéndez Pidal mentions several occurrences of a lion's escape from his cage.

In *Midsummer Night's Dream* (III, 1 and V, 1) there are allusions to a lion in the court of James VII of Scotland. As part of the entertainment on a certain occasion, a chariot bearing several goddesses was to have been drawn into the hall by a tame lion. For fear that such a sight would frighten the ladies, however, the lion was replaced by a lackey. The incident was a joke to the more sophisticated Londoners.

In the Metropolitan Museum of Art there is a bronze statuette of the nature goddess Cybele in a chariot drawn by two lions; it dates from the second century after Christ.

[2] This piece of furniture served both as a couch and a bench; it must have had a fairly high back, for later the poet says Fernando hid *behind* it.

crawled behind the beam of a wine press, soiling his cloak and tunic.

At this moment the Cid awoke, he who was born in a blessed hour. Seeing his couch surrounded by his loyal men, he asked, "What is this? What are you about to do?"

"The lion, honored lord, has given us quite a scare."

The Cid raised himself on one elbow, then got up from the couch. Trailing his cloak from his shoulders, he walked straight up to the lion. When the lion saw him, he was filled with such awe of the Cid that he lowered his head until it rested on the floor. The Cid Don Rodrigo took him by the mane and led him away to put him back in the cage, to the amazement of all present.

When they returned to the hall of the palace, the Cid asked for his sons-in-law, but they were nowhere to be found. Although their names were called repeatedly, no one answered. When they were at last discovered and came before the Cid, with all color drained from their faces, they were the object of the court's mockery, until the Cid put an end to the jests. The Infantes de Carrión considered themselves disgraced and felt great bitterness over the incident.

113

The Infantes continued to lament their situation. Meanwhile, an army from Morocco came to besiege Valencia. They encamped in the adjacent field of Cuarto, raising fifty thousand main tents. The king of this host was named Búcar.

114

The Cid and all his vassals rejoiced and gave thanks to the Creator for this opportunity to increase their fortune. However, the Infantes de Carrión were worried; the sight of so many Moorish tents gave them little pleasure. The two brothers withdrew to discuss the situation. "When we mar-

ried the Cid's daughters, we were thinking only of what we
would gain, and not of what we might lose. There is no way
we can avoid going into this battle. It is certain that we shall
never see Carrión again, and the daughters of the Campeador
will be left widows."

Muño Gustioz overheard their words and went to report
them to the Cid Campeador. "What valiant heroes are those
sons-in-law of yours! Because they are about to go into this
battle, they long to be in Carrión! Go comfort them, for the
love of God. Let them stay out of the fight and have no part
in the battle, for you and the rest of us, with God's help, will
be able to win it."

The Cid Don Rodrigo sought out the Infantes de Carrión
and spoke to them with a smile on his lips, "God save you,
my sons! In your embrace you hold my daughters, fair as the
sun. While I thirst for battle, you long for Carrión. Stay here
in Valencia, then, and take your leisure to your heart's con-
tent. I know how to handle those Moors; God will give me
the courage to rout them."

115

[While [3] they were talking thus, a message arrived from
King Búcar warning the Cid either to give up Valencia and
withdraw peacefully or give satisfaction for the offenses he
had committed against the Moroccan King. The Cid sent
the messenger back with the following reply: "Go tell
Búcar, that son of an enemy, that before three days have
passed I shall have given him the satisfaction he demands."

The next day the Cid ordered all his men to prepare for
battle, and they rode out against the Moors. The Infantes
de Carrión asked to lead the charge. And so, when the Cid
had drawn up his lines of battle, one of the Infantes, Don
Fernando, rode forth to attack a Moor named Aladraf. The

[3] One sheet of the manuscript is missing here; the details of the fifty-
line lacuna are supplied from the corresponding section of the prose ver-
sion of the *Chronicle of Twenty Kings*.

Moor in turn came at him on sight. The terrified Infante
did not have the courage to hold his ground and engage
him in single combat but jerked his horse around and fled.

Pedro Bermúdez, who was riding close at hand, saw what
had happened; at once he rode at the Moor, engaged him,
and slew him. Then he caught the Moor's horse, rode after
the fleeing Infante, and said to him, "Don Fernando, take
this horse and tell everybody that you killed its Moorish
owner; I shall swear that I witnessed the feat."

"Don Pedro Bermúdez," said the Infante, "I thank you
for those words.]

May I live to repay you twice over."

The two rode back together, and Don Pedro lent his author-
ity to the deed of which Fernando boasted. The Cid and all
his vassals were pleased.

"God in heaven willing, both my sons-in-law will prove to
be valiant in combat!"

Meanwhile, they kept advancing on the enemy amidst the
din of the Moorish drums, a sound which awed many of those
Christian knights who had recently joined the Cid and had
never heard it before. But the most overawed of all were
Diego and Fernando, who, if they had had their wish, would
have been far away from there.

The Cid, born in a blessed hour, called out, "Ho, Pedro
Bermúdez, my dear nephew, see to the safety of my sons-in-
law Diego and Fernando, for I prize them highly. If God
favors us, the Moors will not long hold the field!"

116

"By the love of God, O Cid," swore Pedro Bermúdez, "to-
day I will not take care of the Infantes! Let somebody else
do it; I care nothing about them. I want to be at the head of
the assault with my men, while you and yours should hold
fast in the rear to come to my quick support if the need
should arise."

Then Minaya Álvar Fáñez came up. "Hear me, O Cid,

loyal Campeador! The Creator will take a hand in this battle, and so will you, who have always enjoyed so worthily his favor. Tell us from what direction you want us to attack, and every one of us will do his duty. Then with God's help and with your usual good fortune we shall see how the battle turns out."

Said the Cid, "Let us not act with too much haste."

Then Bishop Don Jerónimo, splendidly armed, appeared before the heaven-favored Cid and spoke, "This morning I sang the Mass of the Holy Trinity for you. I abandoned my country and came here to join you only because I desired to slay Moors. I yearn to bring glory upon my arms and my religious order and I seek the privilege of striking the first blows of the battle. With the consent of God I should like to put to the test these arms I bear, with the figures of deer on my pennant and my own insigne. Thus would I content my heart and heighten your esteem for me, O Cid. And if you do not grant me this request, I am determined to leave your company."

Then spoke the Cid, "I am pleased to grant what you wish. But here come the Moors; go forth to attack them, and from here we shall see how the Bishop performs in combat."

117

Bishop Don Jerónimo spurred out to attack the Moors, his charge taking him to the far end of their camp. Through his own good fortune and by the grace of God whose favor the Bishop enjoyed, he killed two Moors with the first blows of the battle. Having broken his lance, he drew his sword and performed heroically. God, how that Bishop did fight! He had killed two with the lance and now he slew five others with his sword. Great numbers of Moors surrounded him and landed fierce blows, none of which broke through his defensive armor.

Seeing the Bishop in peril, the Cid, born in a blessed hour, fixed his shield in position, lowered his lance, set spurs to his swift horse Babieca, and attacked with all the ferocity of his heart and soul. He broke through their front lines, knocked seven Moors from their steeds, and killed four. Before these feats of arms, a joy to God, the Moors began to retreat, and the Cid and his men sped in pursuit of them. Everywhere tent ropes snapped, stakes were pulled out of the ground, and decorated tent poles fell to earth. The Cid's men forced Búcar and his host to yield their camp.

118

Driving them from the camp, the Cid's men again took up the pursuit. Here and there lay an arm slashed off, still wearing its sleeve of armor; many a head, still wearing its helmet, rolled to the ground; riderless chargers fled the field in every direction. The chase went on for seven miles.

The Cid, riding in pursuit of King Búcar, called out, "Turn back, Búcar! You have come from across the sea and now you shall settle matters with the Cid of the long beard. Let us give each other a sign of friendship and form a bond of peace."

Búcar replied to the Cid, "God confound such a peace as you offer! I can see that sword in your hand as you gallop toward me, and I do not doubt that you intend to try it out on me. But unless my horse stumbles and falls with me, you will have to ride into the sea to catch me."

"Not so!" the Cid answered.

Although Búcar's horse was a splendid animal and was covering ground swiftly, the Cid's Babieca kept closing in on him. The Cid finally overtook Búcar about six paces from the seashore. He raised his sword Colada and struck the Moor a mighty blow that split the helmet and all, knocking off its decorative knobs, and cut the man's body in two clear to the waist.

The Cid had killed Búcar, the king from across the sea, and he had won the sword Tizón, worth a thousand marks of gold! The Cid had won a great and wondrous victory and brought glory to himself, as had all his vassals!

119

With their plunder, the Christian knights came back from the pursuit and thoroughly stripped the battleground of spoils. A group of them accompanied the Cid Ruy Díaz back to the camp. The illustrious Campeador, carrying the two swords which he prized so highly, rode swiftly through the field strewn with the dead. His hood of mail hung at his shoulders, and his cloth cap, somewhat wrinkled, still covered his hair. The vassals gathered around him from every direction. The Cid raised his eyes and held them fast on a sight which filled his heart with pleasure: the approach of Diego and Fernando, the two sons of the Count Don Gonzalo. A smile of happiness brightened the Cid's face. "Hail, my sons-in-law, my own sons! I can see that you delight in combat. The people of Carrión shall hear of your deeds and of our defeat of King Búcar. I trust in God and all his saints that this victory will be a highly rewarding one."

At this moment Minaya Álvar Fáñez rode up. From his neck was slung his shield, battered and dented from futile blows of sword and from the thrust of many a lance turned aside. He had slain more than twenty Moors, and his arm was drenched with their blood to the elbow. "Thanks be to God on high," he cried, "and to you, O Cid, born in a blessed hour! You have killed Búcar, and we have won the battle. Now all this wealth belongs to you and your vassals. Your sons-in-law, too, have had their fill of battling Moors and have proved strong in combat."

Said the Cid, "I am more than pleased with their action. They are good knights now, and as time goes on they will have few equals."

Although the Cid's words were spoken in all sincerity, the Infantes construed them as mockery.

Then they brought all they had won into Valencia, and the Cid and his vassals rejoiced, for each share was worth six hundred silver marks.

The Cid's sons-in-law, having safely in their possession

their share of the spoils of victory, felt sure that they would never be pressed for money as long as they lived. The people of Valencia were abundantly provided with excellent food, fine furs, and rich clothing. The Cid and his vassals were altogether happy.

120

The victory they had won and the slaying of King Búcar made for a great day in the Campeador's court. Raising his hand to take hold of his beard, he said, "Thanks be to Christ, Lord of the universe! He has granted me to see what I longed for, my two sons-in-law fighting by my side on the field of battle. A worthy account of their conduct will reach the land of Carrión; men will know how they have won glory and that they will ever do us gallant service."

121

The booty they had won was enormous; part of it was given to the men, and the rest was placed in safekeeping. The Cid, born in a blessed hour, ordered each of his knights to take his allotment of the spoils of this victory, and not to overlook the fifth part due the leader. They judiciously complied with the orders. The one-fifth which was the Cid's portion included six hundred horses, as well as innumerable mules and camels.

122

These were the prizes the Campeador had won.

"Thanks be to God, Lord of the world! Not long ago I was impoverished, and now I am rich. I have goods and land and gold and estates. Furthermore, the noble Infantes de Carrión are my sons-in-law. By God's grace, I keep on winning battles; Moors and Christians alike hold me in great fear. Far away in Morocco, land of the mosques, perhaps those Moors fear that I will fall upon them some night. But I do not intend to do so. No, I shall not invade their lands, but rather, with God's help, I will make them pay tribute to me or to whomever I choose, while I stay here in Valencia."

In Valencia there was great rejoicing among the Cid Campeador's company over the victory they had won with such bold hearts. Great also was the joy of both his sons-in-law, the Infantes de Carrión, who together had been enriched to the extent of five thousand marks and thus counted themselves very wealthy.

One day they went in company with others to the Cid's palace, where they found also present Bishop Don Jerónimo; that valiant knight, good Álvar Fáñez; and many others whom the Cid had reared in his home and trained for knighthood. When the Infantes de Carrión entered they were met on behalf of the Cid Campeador by Minaya:

"Come, my kinsmen. We are honored by your presence."

Seeing them come in, the Cid was pleased and said, "Here, my sons-in-law, is my noble wife, and here are my daughters, Doña Elvira and Doña Sol. Let them do your pleasure and attend your every wish. Thanks be to Saint Mary, Mother of our Lord God! Through these marriages you have made, your fortunes will mount, and your fame will soar in the land of Carrión."

123

The Infante Fernando made answer to the Cid's words, "Thanks to the Creator, and to you, O honored Cid, we now have untold wealth; through you we have achieved distinction in successful battle against the Moors and we have killed that proven traitor King Búcar.[4] Now that our own estate is assured, it is time for you to turn your attention to other matters."

The vassals of the Cid, who had fought so gallantly in the recent battle and had taken so conspicuous a part in the pursuit, smiled at these words, for not one of them had seen

4 "Proven traitor" is probably intended as general abuse and does not refer, as far as I know, to a specific act of treachery.

either Diego or Fernando during the action. The ceaseless jibes and bitter mockery of the vassals drove the Infantes to contrive a devilish plot. Drawing aside, the two brothers, one as bad as the other, made their inhumanly foul plans.

"Let us go back to Carrión; we have tarried here too long. Our wealth is now so great that it will more than suffice us for the rest of our lives.

124

"Let us ask the Cid Campeador for our wives; we shall say that we wish to take them to the land of Carrión so that we may show them the country where their estates lie. In this way we can get them out of Valencia and away from the protection of the Campeador; then, during the trip, we shall do as we please with them, before somebody taunts us again about that lion incident. In our veins flows the blood of the Counts of Carrión! We shall take with us immeasurable wealth, and at the same time we shall dishonor the Cid's daughters.

"With all this wealth we shall become grandees, in a position to marry the daughters of kings or emperors, for our family is that of the Counts of Carrión. This is the way we shall mock the daughters of the Campeador—before somebody can ridicule us again over the lion episode!"

Their plans laid, they returned to the court, where Fernando González obtained silence in order to speak. "God protect you, Cid Campeador! May it please Doña Jimena, and you first of all, O Cid, and Minaya Álvar Fáñez, and all present to permit us to take our duly married wives to our land of Carrión, where they may come into possession of the estates we gave them as a wedding endowment; there your daughters will inspect our patrimony, which will fall to the children we may have in the future."

The Cid, suspecting no treachery, replied, "I give you my daughters, and in addition a part of my treasure. You have given them marriage gifts of villas in the land of Carrión; I wish to give them a dowry of three thousand marks. To you I shall give mules and palfreys of surpassing size and quality, and strong, swift chargers, and many raiments woven of silk and gold. I shall give you the two swords, Colada and Tizón, which I won through manly combat, as you well know. You are truly my own sons, for I have given my daughters to you; you are taking part of my heart away when you take them from me. Let all Galicia and Castile and León know the rich farewell I give my sons-in-law. Attend with every care my daughters who are now your wives, and I shall reward you well."

The Infantes de Carrión gave their word, and the Campeador's daughters were handed over to them. Then began the presentation of the gifts the Cid had offered.

Having been given everything they could desire, the Infantes de Carrión ordered it all packed and loaded. There was great activity in the city of Valencia; knights in full regalia swiftly mounted their chargers to ride out with the Cid's daughters and send them off with pomp to the land of Carrión.

As they prepared to ride away, the two sisters, Doña Elvira and Doña Sol, knelt in leave-taking before the Cid Campeador.

"May God avail you, Father! We ask of you a favor, kneeling before you, our father and our mother who gave us life. Now you are sending us to the land of Carrión, and it is our duty to obey. But we ask of you this favor, that you send news of you to us in the land of Carrión."

The Cid embraced them and kissed them.

125

The mother then added her loving farewell to the father's. "Go, then, my daughters, and may God ever watch over you! Know that you will always have your father's love and mine. Go to Carrión, to the estates acquired through what I feel is a fine marriage."

They kissed the hands of their mother and father and received their love and blessing.

The Cid and his men rode out, forming a colorful parade of knights in full armor on splendidly caparisoned horses. Now the Infantes left fair Valencia after saying good-by to their companions and to the ladies in waiting. The Cid and all his company of knights rode festively through the Garden of Valencia sporting their arms.

But the Cid, who girt the sword in a blessed hour, foresaw from certain omens that these marriages would not be entirely successful. Yet it was too late to alter anything; his daughters were already married.

126

"O Félix Muñoz, my nephew and the dearest cousin of my two daughters! I want you to go with them to Carrión to see the estates which have been given them; then you will come back and report to me."

"Gladly will I do so," replied Félix Muñoz.

Minaya Álvar Fáñez appeared before the Cid. "Let us ride back to Valencia, O Cid, for with the sanction of God the Spiritual Father, we shall some day go to visit them in the land of Carrión."

"We entrust you to God's care, Doña Elvira and Doña Sol. Let everything you do bring pride to us."

"May God so will," replied the sons-in-law.

Great was the sorrow of their parting; father and daughters wept with profound feeling, and the knights of the Campeador shared in the grief.

"Hear me, my nephew Félix Muñoz!" the Cid called out. "You are to go to Molina, where you will spend the night. Give my greetings to my good ally Abengalbón, the Moor, and ask him to receive my sons-in-law with all hospitality. Tell him that I am sending my daughters to the land of Carrión; bid him, out of regard for me, provide for their every need and escort them as far as Medinaceli. Let him know that I shall reward him abundantly for all he may do for them."

Then came the parting, as painful as tearing a nail from the flesh of the finger. The Cid, born in a blessed hour, returned to Valencia, and the Infantes de Carrión rode on their way. They stopped overnight at Santa María de Albarracín, then continued their swift pace until they came to Molina where the Moor Abengalbón was lord. The Moor was highly pleased to learn of their arrival, and he came out to offer them a joyous welcome. At his castle he afforded them every hospitality they could wish for. The next morning he joined the travelers with an escort of two hundred knights under his command. They passed through the wooded country called Luzón and the Valley of Arbujuelo, and came to the river Jalón, where they halted at a place called Ansarera. There the Moor, out of regard for the Cid Campeador, offered presents to the Cid's daughters, and to each of the Infantes de Carrión he gave a fine charger.

But the two brothers, seeing the rich presents which the Moor had brought forth, concocted an act of treachery. "Since we are going to desert the Cid's daughters anyway, we might as well kill the Moor, Abengalbón, too, if we can, and have all that wealth for ourselves. We could keep it as secure as our estates in Carrión, and we shall never have to answer to the Cid for our actions."

But a certain Moor who knew their language overheard the villainous scheme of the Infantes de Carrión and straightway revealed it to Abengalbón. "My lord Abengalbón, beware of those two, for I heard them plotting your death."

127

With his two hundred knights the Moor Abengalbón, a bold young man, rode up to the Infantes, holding his arms of battle in threatening fashion. The words he spoke held no delight for them. "If it were not for the respect I bear for the

Cid of Vivar, I would strike you both such blows that the sound would be heard throughout the world! Then I would return the loyal Campeador's daughters to him, and you would never again set foot on the soil of Carrión.

128

"Tell me, Infantes de Carrión, what wrong have I ever done you? While I was doing you a service in all good faith, you plotted my death. Not one step farther will I accompany you, evil traitors. With your permission, Doña Elvira and Doña Sol, I shall leave. The renowned Infantes de Carrión are contemptible in my sight. May God, Lord of the world, be pleased to grant that the Cid may never regret your marriages."

Saying this, the Moor turned about and rode back across the river Jalón, still brandishing his arms. With ample justification he returned to Molina.

Then the Infantes de Carrión set out from Ansarera, traveling night and day. They passed to the right of Atienza, located on a strongly fortified hill, then crossed the Sierra de Miedes and rode swiftly through Montes Claros; [5] they passed to the right of Griza, founded by Álamos; there are located the caves where they say Álamos kept a certain Elfa imprisoned.[6] Farther on to their right was San Esteban.

At length the Infantes entered an oak forest named Corpes, where the trees are so lofty their branches tower into the clouds and where wild animals roam. Coming upon a fresh spring in a flowered clearing, the Infantes ordered their tents pitched, and there the entire company spent the night. The Infantes, lying with their wives in their embrace, poured forth warm endearments.

But at sunrise their words of love are evilly belied. They

[5] This is not, of course, the previously mentioned Montes Claros in Africa; it is in the province of Guadalajara, Spain. Montes Claros appears as a place name in several other provinces of Spain.

[6] Both Álamos and Elfa are unknown to history and must belong to the local—and now forgotten—legend alluded to here.

give orders for the abundant treasure to be loaded on the pack animals and the tent where they have spent the night to be struck. The Infantes de Carrión have sent ahead everyone in the band on the express orders that no one, neither man nor woman, remain behind except their wives Doña Elvira and Doña Sol, with whom they wish to be free to enjoy themselves.

As soon as the others have gone ahead, and the four are left alone, the Infantes turn to their brutal act.

"Of a certainty, Doña Elvira and Doña Sol, in this forbidding wilderness we are going to make a mockery of you. Today we are going on, and we shall desert you here; you will never come into possession of your estates in Carrión. When the Cid Campeador hears of what we have done, then shall we have our revenge for that incident of the lion."

Then they rip off the girls' cloaks and furs, leaving them covered only by tunic and blouse.[7] When the ladies see their treacherous husbands standing over them wearing spurs and clutching great heavy leather cinches in their hands, Doña Elvira cries out, "In God's name, Don Diego and Don Fernando! You have two swords, strong and keen, Colada and Tizón. Make martyrs of us by cutting off our heads. Moors and Christians alike will loathe your deed and say that we have not deserved this fate. Do not torture us, for you will only cheapen yourselves by wronging us, and you will have to give satisfaction in a court of justice."

[7] The selection of appropriate American English terms for medieval articles of clothing is almost as baffling as would be the task of translating "bobby-sox" or "slim-jims" into Medieval Spanish. Nevertheless, I shall attempt (with little confidence of achieving absolute accuracy) to indicate what the ladies of *The Cid* may have worn, from the inside out. The innermost garment was the *camisa,* a chemise or blouse which covered the torso. Over this was worn the *brial* or *ciclatón,* a long tunic vaguely comparable to a modern underskirt or petticoat—with sleeves, however; it was visible. The *piel* or *pellizón* was a somewhat shorter kind of tunic made of fur covered with cloth. In this translation the term "fur" is used for this garment. The *manto* was a mantle or cloak.

There seems to have been little essential difference in the court costumes of men and women.

But the girls' pleading is futile. The Infantes de Carrión begin to beat them cruelly with the buckles of the straps; with their sharp spurs, they rake them painfully, tearing their clothing and their flesh, so that the bright blood stains their tunics.

Anguish now tears at the girls' hearts. O, how fortunate if, God willing, the Cid Campeador should suddenly appear!

So cruelly have they been beaten that they lie helpless, their clothing soaked with blood. At last the two Infantes, each trying to outdo the other in the ferocity of his blows, tire of the sport. Doña Elvira and Doña Sol, no longer able to speak, are left for dead in the Forest of Corpes.

129

They strip them of their cloaks and their furs of ermine, leaving the beaten girls half-dressed in blouse and tunic, at the mercy of the birds of the forest and the wild animals. Then they abandon them for dead, without life. O, what great fortune if only the Cid Ruy Díaz should appear at that moment!

130

The Infantes de Carrión think them dead, for neither girl makes a move to help the other. As they make their way through the forest they boast of what they have done. "Now we have had revenge for our marriages. We should never have taken those women even for concubines if we hadn't been begged; they were too far below us in station to be our wives. Now the humiliation of that lion affair has been avenged."

131

Thus the Infantes de Carrión boasted.

But Félix Muñoz, the Cid's nephew, had been very reluctant to ride on ahead when ordered to do so. Pricked by a certain suspicion, he drew apart from the others and entered a thicket in order to watch for his cousins to pass by and to discover what the Infantes de Carrión had done. He saw the latter coming and was able to hear what they said. They could not see him, nor did they even suspect his presence; if they had, he would certainly not have escaped with his life.

When the Infantes had galloped past, Félix Muñoz rode back along the route and found his cousins, both of them unconscious. Crying out, "My cousins, my cousins!" he leaped to the ground, tethered his mount, and ran to them.

"My cousins, my cousins! Doña Elvira and Doña Sol! What wickedness have the Infantes de Carrión done! May God give them the reward they deserve for this!"

Gradually, he began to revive them. The girls were in such a deep faint that they could not utter a word. His heart was wrenched by the sight of them.

"My cousins, my cousins!" he called to them. "Doña Elvira! Doña Sol! For the love of God, wake up, cousins, while it is still light, before night falls, or we will be eaten by the wild beasts of the forest."

Little by little, Doña Elvira and Doña Sol were recovering their senses; they opened their eyes and saw Félix Muñoz.

"Gather your strength, my cousins," he begged them. "As soon as the Infantes de Carrión discover my absence, they will come after me in all haste, and unless God protects us, we shall die on the spot."

With great pain, Doña Elvira spoke, "For the love of God, give us water, and may my father the Campeador repay your kindness."

In a fine hat, which he had just brought from Valencia, Félix Muñoz brought water and gave it to his cousins and slaked the thirst induced by their severe wounds.

Pleading with them, he managed to bring them to a sitting position. He encouraged and comforted them until they felt stronger; at once he placed them both on his horse and covered them with his cloak, took the horse by the reins, and set out. Through the Forest of Corpes the three made their

forlorn way, coming out of it at the hour when day gives way
to night. When they reached the river Duero, Félix Muñoz
left the two girls at the Torre de Doña Urraca. Then he went
to San Esteban de Gormaz, where he sought out Diego Téllez,
a vassal of Álvar Fáñez. When Diego Téllez learned what had
happened to the Cid's daughters, his heart was grieved. He
went out to receive Doña Elvira and Doña Sol with horses and
decent clothing. Then he put them up in San Esteban, where
he paid them every possible respect and attention. The people
of San Esteban, always known for their kindness, were filled
with pity on hearing of the atrocity done to the Cid's daugh-
ters, and they brought them tribute of meat, grain, and wine.[8]
The girls stayed in San Esteban until they recovered.

Meanwhile, the Infantes de Carrión continued to boast.
What they had done became known in every part of the
country. The good King Alfonso was extremely shocked. When
the report of the deed reached Valencia and the ears of the
Cid Campeador, he remained for a long time in deep thought.
Raising his hand to his beard, he declared, "Praise be to
Christ, Lord of the world! This is the way the Infantes de
Carrión have chosen to honor me! I swear by this beard,
which no man has ever touched in insult, that their deed will
little avail the Infantes de Carrión, for I shall see that my
daughters have the sort of marriage they deserve."

The Cid's heart was torn with anguish, and his entire court,
particularly Álvar Fáñez, shared his grief.

Álvar Fáñez set out on horse with Pedro Bermúdez, the
illustrious Martín Antolínez of Burgos, and two hundred other
knights sent by the Cid, who had ordered them to travel day
and night and bring his daughters back to Valencia. Without
delay and as ordered by their lord, they rode hard day and

----

[8] San Esteban was under tribute to Álvar Fáñez and its people were
obliged to bring him yearly offerings from their land. Since Álvar Fáñez,
in turn, was a vassal of the Cid, the gifts to the Cid's daughters might
represent an indirect form of payment to Álvar Fáñez. It seems more
likely that in this instance they acted purely out of charitable motives.

night. They reached Gormaz, a strongly fortified castle, and spent the night there. When it was reported at San Esteban that Minaya was coming for his cousins, the worthy men of the town came out to receive Minaya and his company, and that night they presented him with abundant tokens of their fealty. Minaya refused to accept these offerings, but he thanked them warmly. "My thanks, worthy men of San Esteban, for the honored service you have lent us in this misfortune. And I thank you on behalf of the Cid Campeador, who, in Valencia, is as grateful to you as am I, here in your presence. May God in his heaven grant you a just reward for your services."

Those of San Esteban were pleased by Minaya's air and expressed their appreciation. Then they went home for their nightly rest, while Minaya went to see his cousins, Doña Elvira and Doña Sol. When they set eyes on him they cried out that they were as glad to see him as if he were the Lord himself. "You may thank God that we are alive. In Valencia, when the shock has worn off, we shall tell you the whole story of our misfortune."

132

The ladies and Álvar Fáñez were shedding tears, as was Pedro Bermúdez. "Doña Elvira and Doña Sol," said the latter, "make an end of your grief, for now you are well and alive, and your trials are past. You have lost husbands of noble rank, but perhaps you will be wed again to an even loftier station. And I hope the day of vengeance is yet to come!"

There with gladdened hearts they spent the night. The next morning when they began the return trip to Valencia, the people of San Esteban rode out to keep them company on the road as far as Riodamor; there, saying good-by to the travelers, they turned back, and Minaya continued on his way with the ladies. They passed through Alcoceva, to the left of Gormaz, through the village called Vadorrey, and stopped overnight in the town of Berlanga. Resuming their journey the next morning, they halted for the night in Medinaceli. The next day's ride brought them from there to Molina, where the Moor Abengalbón showed his pleasure at their arrival by going out to welcome them heartily. Out of honor to the Cid, he made them his guests at a rich banquet. Afterwards, they proceeded straight toward Valencia.

When the Cid, born in a blessed hour, was informed of their approach, he mounted at once and rode out to receive them, festively playing his weapons in expression of the joy he felt. He embraced his daughters and kissed them, then spoke with a glad smile. "And so, you have come, my daughters! God keep you from further harm! I had to approve those marriages of yours, for I dared not speak out against them. I pray God on high to see you married more worthily, and may he grant me vengeance on my sons-in-law the Infantes de Carrión!"

The daughters kissed their father's hands, and with the knights playing their arms they entered the city, where the mother Doña Jimena received her daughters joyously.

Losing no time, the Cid held council with his vassals and decided to send his representative to King Alfonso of Castile.

<h2 style="text-align:center">133</h2>

"O Muño Gustioz, my illustrious vassal! Glad am I that I raised you in my household. You will take a message to Castile for King Alfonso. In my name, kiss his hand in earnest token that I hold myself his vassal and acknowledge him as my lord. Let the good King suffer as deeply as I do from this insult the Infantes de Carrión have done me. The King is the one who gave my daughters in marriage, not I, and now that they have been dishonored, whatever affront has been done to me, whether great or small, concerns my lord as well. They have wronged and incensed me further by keeping the money and the other gifts I gave them. Ask the King to summon the Infantes de Carrión to a trial of justice [9] so that I may have satisfaction from them, for bitter is the anger within my heart."

Muño Gustioz set out immediately, accompanied by two knights, who were to serve him diligently, and several squires of his household. From Valencia they rode as fast as they could, stopping neither day nor night to rest. In Sahagún they found Don Alfonso, King of Castile, of León, Asturias, and San Salvador; his realm extended even to Santiago, where Galician counts held him to be their lord. Muño Gustioz dismounted, knelt in homage to the saints, and offered a prayer to God. Then he proceeded with his attending knights to the palace of the King's court.

As they entered the hall, the King recognized Muño Gustioz on sight; he rose and greeted the party courteously. Muño Gustioz knelt before the King and kissed his feet.

"Hail, O King, lord of far-flung realms! The Campeador kisses your hands and feet; he is your vassal, and you are his lord. You gave his daughters in marriage to the Infantes de Carrión, thus lending honor to the marriage by your interest. By now you have heard of the 'honor' the marriage has brought our family, of the atrocity which the Infantes de Carrión have committed. They have vilely beaten the daughters of the Cid Campeador, leaving them in the Forest of Corpes with torn flesh and half naked, dishonored, abandoned as prey to the birds and savage animals of the wild. Now his daughters are in Valencia.

"Therefore, your vassal the Cid begs you, as his lord, to summon the Infantes to a court of justice. He regards himself as gravely insulted, but you have been insulted in a

---

[9] These courts of justice (Medieval Spanish *aiuntas* or *iuntas, vistas, cortes*) were assemblies of the judicial officers of the district concerned. The king himself sometimes presided over the *cortes*, as is the case in *The Cid*. Litigation was frequently resolved by decree of the presiding official, but many an afternoon was brightened for the populace by the colorful spectacle of trial by combat; it was especially used when the case was of major importance. The participants had to adhere to a system of rules, procedures, and conventions as rigid and complex as those prescribed for the bullfight or major league baseball. (Cf. note p. 111.)

greater degree. O wise King, let the Cid's grievance be your
own. Grant that the Cid may have satisfaction of the In-
fantes de Carrión."

For a long time the King remained silent in thought. At
last he spoke, "Indeed, my heart is grieved, and it is true, as
you say, that I am the one who gave his daughters in marriage
to the Infantes de Carrión; I acted in the good faith that the
match would be of advantage to the Cid. Would today that
the marriages, which have brought such anguish to me and to
the Cid, had never taken place! By my hope of salvation, I
promise to help him obtain justice. Although I was not
planning to do so at the present time, I shall send my heralds
throughout the kingdom to announce a session of the royal
court in Toledo; there let the counts and other noblemen
assemble. I shall order the Infantes to appear and give satis-
faction to the Cid Campeador. The Cid shall suffer no
grievance for long if I can prevent it.

134

"Tell the Campeador, born in a blessed hour, that I grant
him and his vassals a period of seven weeks from today in
which to prepare to come to Toledo. I am calling this court
on behalf of the Cid. In my name convey greetings to him
and his vassals, and bid them be of good cheer, for from this
affront a measure of honor may still come to them."

Muño Gustioz took leave of the King and returned to the
Cid.

Just as he had said, Alfonso the Castilian took the matter
for his own concern. At once the honored King sent messages
to León and to Santiago, to the Portuguese and to the
Galicians, to the men of Carrión and of Castile, ordering all
to attend a court which would be held in Toledo in seven
weeks; whoever should fail to appear would no longer be
regarded as vassals of the King. Throughout the realm, his
vassals determined to comply with the orders of the King.

135

The Infantes de Carrión were filled with apprehension at the fact that the King had called a court of justice, for they feared that the Cid Campeador would have a part in it. They sought the counsel of their kinsmen and were advised to beg that the King excuse them from this court.

Replied the King, "No, so help me God, I will not! The Cid Campeador will be here, and you must give him satisfaction for the grievance he bears against you. If either of you fails to appear at the court or refuses satisfaction to the Cid, he shall lose my favor and be ordered to leave the kingdom."

To the Infantes de Carrión it was clear that there was no escape. Again, they took counsel with their relatives, among them Count Don García Ordóñez, an enemy of the Cid who sought every chance to harm him; he was to act as the Infantes' adviser.

The appointed day of the court was drawing near, and the people began to assemble. Among the first to arrive were the good King Alfonso, Count Don Enrique, Count Don Remond, who was the father of the good emperor, and Counts Don Froila and Don Birbón.[10] In attendance at the court were all of those most highly skilled in legal procedure in all Castile. Also present were Count Don García, called El Crespo de Grañón, and Álvar Díaz, lord of Oca; Asur González, Gonzalo Ansúrez; and Pedro Ansúrez; as well as Diego and Fernando,

[10] The Counts Enrique, Remond, and Froila are King Alfonso's judges, or magistrates, of the trial which will decide the issue between the Cid and the Infantes de Carrión. Enrique is the cousin of Queen Constanza, Alfonso's wife, and also the King's son-in-law, having married a natural daughter of Alfonso. Remond is the husband of the King's legitimate daughter Urraca; the "good emperor" referred to is Alfonso VII, the son of this couple. Froila is the Cid's brother-in-law and the *mayordomo* of Count Remond. There is some doubt about the identity of Count Birbón, and even about the correct form of his name.

Following mention of these noblemen are listed some of the Carrión partisans, none of whom serve as judges.

who had brought a great band of their kinsmen to the court
with the intention of using force against the Cid Campeador.

From everywhere the people gathered; and yet the Cid,
born in a blessed hour, had not yet made his appearance,
and his delay was beginning to annoy the King. On the fifth
day the Cid Campeador arrived in the city. He sent Álvar
Fáñez to kiss the hands of the King, his lord, and to inform
him that he would be there by nightfall. The King, pleased
to hear this, mounted his steed and rode out with a great
retinue to receive his vassal. The Cid and his men were
attired in splendid regalia, a worthy company for a worthy
lord.

As soon as he came within sight of good King Alfonso, the
Cid Campeador leaped to the ground and began to humble
himself before his lord and to do him honor, but at once, the
King protested. "By Saint Isidore, I shall have none of this!
Get back on your horse, O Cid, if you do not wish to dis-
please me, and we shall exchange sincere greetings on equal
terms. Know that the trouble which afflicts your heart is my
own as well. May God grant that this court be honored to-
day through you."

"Amen!" added the noble Cid Campeador. He kissed the
King's hand and then his lips. "I am thankful to be in your
presence, praise God. My respects to you, to the Counts Don
Remond and Don Enrique, and to all the others present.
God save you, my lord, and all our friends! My good wife,
Doña Jimena, and my two daughters beg you to take to heart
the affliction which has fallen upon us."

Replied the King, "So help me God, I do!"

136

The King started back to Toledo, but the Cid did not
want to cross the river Tajo that night. "God save you, O
King; grant me a favor," he asked. "While you go on into
the city of Toledo, let me and my men remain for the night
in the monastery of San Servando. There the rest of my com-

pany will join me tonight. I shall keep vigil [11] in that holy place and tomorrow morning I shall come to Toledo and appear at the court before noon."

The King willingly granted his request and returned to Toledo, while the Cid Ruy Díaz went to pass the night at San Servando. There he had candles lighted and placed on the altar, and there in that holy place spent the night in lonely prayer and communion with God, as had been his desire.

By morning, Minaya and the goodly knights of the company were ready for the work that lay before them.

137

They said their matins and heard mass before the sun came up, leaving a handsome offering.

"You, Minaya Álvar Fáñez, my strong right arm, will go with me. And you, Bishop Don Jerónimo, and Pedro Bermúdez, and Muño Gustioz, and you too, Martín Antolínez, O famous knight of Burgos, and Álvar Álvarez, Álvar Salvadórez, Martín Muñoz, of propitious time of birth, and my nephew Félix Muñoz, the learned Mal Anda, and the good knight Galindo García of Aragón. Enough of my other valiant knights will be selected to make us a hundred strong. All of you are first to put on tunics [12] to protect against the discomfort of the armor; then don the coat of mail, bright as the flashing sun; then, over the mail, your ermine tunics, well fastened so that the armor cannot be seen; under the mantles you will wear your swords, well-tempered and keen. I shall go

---

[11] Keeping vigil involved spending the whole night in prayer in a holy place before a battle or other impending crisis. It ended with morning prayers, mass, and offering. One who was to be dubbed a knight had to spend the night before the ceremony standing vigil (perhaps "standing" literally, or at least kneeling) over his arms, as did a renowned *caballero* by the name of Don Quixote.

[12] *Velmezes* is rendered here as "tunic" because there is no exact equivalent in twentieth-century American English. It may have been a sweatshirt or a quilted slip of some kind.

to the trial thus, with my company fully armed, to demand
my rights and to present my case. If the Infantes de Carrión
attempt treachery, I shall feel secure with such a hundred
men as you around me."

All declared their eagerness to comply with his wishes, and
they dressed and armed themselves exactly as he had in-
structed.

Without delay the Cid, born in a favored hour, put on
breeches of good cloth and a pair of beautifully worked
boots; next, a shirt of fine material, white as the sun, with
gold and silver fasteners down the front and on the cuffs,[13] as
he had ordered them made. Over the shirt he donned a
beautiful tunic of silk brocaded with gold, so that it sparkled
brilliantly; then, a crimson cloak of fur which the Cid always
wore, and a sash of gold. So that no one might have a chance
to insult him by pulling his hair, he covered his head with a
fine linen cap embroidered with gold; for the same reasons
of precaution he bound up his long beard with a cord. His
outer garment was a mantle of great value, a thing of striking
beauty.

And so arrayed, and followed by his hundred knights, who
were dressed and armed in accordance with his instructions,
he rode swiftly from San Servando to the court.

At the outer door he solemnly dismounted and entered
with dignity, surrounded on all sides by his men.

As soon as the Cid appeared, the good King Don Alfonso
rose, as did the Counts Don Enrique and Don Remond and
then the others present, receiving the Cid with the utmost
courtesy. But García Ordóñez and the rest of the Carrión
faction refused to rise.

The King took the Cid by the hands. "Come here and sit by
my side, O Campeador, on this bench which you gave me as a
gift. Your presence does us honor, although to certain ones it
may be displeasing."

[13] There is some doubt of the precise meaning and grammatical struc-
ture of this line. Other translators differ widely in their renditions.
Menéndez Pidal does not comment.

Then the conqueror of Valencia thanked the King effusively. "Keep your seat, as befits a lordly king. I shall sit here among these knights of mine."

The King deferred to the preference of the Cid, who sat down on a bench of turned wood; his men took seats around him. The entire assembly gazed in wonder at the Cid and at his long beard bound up with a cord. What a manly appearance indeed he made in his splendid array! But the Infantes de Carrión turned their eyes away in shame.

At this point the good King Don Alfonso rose. "Hear my words, my vassals, and may the Lord protect you! In the time that I have been king I have called two courts of justice: one in Burgos and the other in Carrión; today I have come to the city of Toledo to hold the third one on behalf of the Cid, born in a blessed hour, so that he may receive satisfaction from the Infantes de Carrión. We all know well the grave wrong they have done him. The judges of the trial will be the Counts Don Enrique and Don Remond and those of you other counts who are not of the Carrión faction. Let all of you consider the case carefully, and let your prudence decide what is right, for I want no injustice done. Let every man of both parties hold his peace. I swear by Saint Isidore that whoever makes a disturbance in my court shall incur my displeasure and be banished from my kingdom. I shall be on the side of whoever proves to be in the right. Now, let the Cid Campeador present his claims; then we shall hear how the Infantes de Carrión make answer."

The Cid knelt to kiss the King's hand and then got to his feet. "I am grateful to you, my lord and King, for convening this court on my behalf. As for the demand I make upon the Infantes de Carrión: the fact that they abandoned my daughters does no dishonor to me, for you, O King, are the one who arranged their marriage and you are the one who will determine what action must be taken today. But when the Infantes de Carrión left Valencia, taking my daughters with them, they enjoyed my sincere affection, and I gave them two swords, Colada and Tizón, which I had won in knightly combat; with these swords I expected them to win renown for themselves in your service. Now, by abandoning my daughters in the Forest of Corpes they have shown that they want nothing that belongs to me, and I have withdrawn my love. Since they are no longer my sons-in-law, let them return my swords."

The judges conceded that the Cid's demand was just.

Count Don García said that his party would answer in a moment. The Infantes de Carrión drew aside for a hurried discussion with their relatives and the others of their group to formulate their reply.

"Certainly the Cid Campeador is acting with restraint in that he does not bring us into account today for the dishonor done to his daughters; we can probably reach a satisfactory settlement of this score with the King Don Alfonso. Let us give the swords back to the Cid, since this is his only demand; then, as soon as he gets them, the trial will be over, and the Cid can make no further claims against us."

Then they returned to the court to state their reply. "Hail, King Don Alfonso, our lord! We cannot deny that the Cid gave us the two swords; since he wants to have them back and demands their return, we agree, with you as our witness, to let him have them."

They took out the swords Colada and Tizón and put them in the hands of the King, their lord. Gleams of light flashed through the hall when the swords were unsheathed, for the knob and the guard of each hilt were of pure gold, and the good men of the court were struck with wonder at the sight. The King called the Cid to him and gave him the swords. Taking them, the Cid kissed the King's hands and returned to the bench from which he had risen. He held the swords in his hands and examined each of them carefully; he knew them too well to be deceived by any substitution on the part of the Infantes. Joy spread throughout his heart and body, and a smile appeared on his face. He raised his hand to take hold of his beard and spoke, "By this beard of mine, which no man has ever dishonored by pulling a single hair, now we shall proceed to avenge Doña Elvira and Doña Sol."

Calling out the name of his nephew Don Pedro Bermúdez he stretched forth his arm and gave him the sword Tizón. "Take it, my nephew," he said; "the sword now has a more worthy owner."

Then to Martín Antolínez, the illustrious knight of Burgos, he offered Colada in his outstretched hand. "Martín Antolínez, O loyal vassal of mine, take Colada. I won it from an excellent master, Don Ramón Berenguer, Count of Barcelona, and for that reason I give it to you. Cherish it well, for I know that when the occasion presents itself you will win great renown and esteem with it."

Kissing the Cid's hand, Martín Antolínez accepted the sword.

Then the Cid Campeador rose and spoke, "Thanks to God, and thanks to you, my lord and King, my request for the return of the swords Colada and Tizón has been granted. Yet another demand for satisfaction I wish to make upon the Infantes de Carrión: When they took my two daughters from Valencia, I gave them three thousand marks of gold and silver; in return for my kindness they committed their barbarous deed. Let them give me back the money, now that they are no longer my sons-in-law."

Thereupon the Infantes began to complain bitterly. When the Count Don Remond ordered them to speak to one effect or the other, the Infantes de Carrión answered, "That is why we gave the Cid Campeador his swords, so that he would make no further claims on us. The return of the swords was the only thing he demanded."

Then came the response of the Count Don Remond, "Subject to the King's approval, we decree as follows: You shall comply with the Cid's demand."

The good King approved the judgment.

Again, the Cid Campeador arose and asked, "Tell me, will you return my money or show just cause for keeping it?"

And again the Infantes de Carrión drew aside to confer privately, but they found no means of complying, for there was a vast amount of money involved, and they had spent it. To the court they made known their decision and told what they proposed to do. "The conqueror of Valencia is making this oppressive claim on us because he covets our fortune so greatly. Very well, we agree to pay him out of the income from our estates in Carrión."

At this confession that they did indeed owe the debt, the judges declared, "If this offer is acceptable to the Cid, we shall not set it aside. But it is our opinion, and we so decree, that you must repay him here in this hall of justice."

To these words King Don Alfonso added his own, "All of us know that in this suit the Cid Campeador is seeking his rights. I myself have two hundred of the three thousand marks; the Infantes gave this amount to me as a gift for my part in their weddings. Now that they find themselves in such straits, I am willing to give back the money to them so that they may pay it to the Cid, born in a blessed hour. I do not wish to keep a part of the dowry which they are obliged to return."

Fernando González declared that the Carrión family had no cash available.

Then the Count Don Remond replied, "You have spent the gold and silver. Our decree, given in the presence of the King Don Alfonso, is that the Infantes are to pay the debt in goods, and that the Cid is to accept such payment."

The Infantes, realizing that there was no course other than to comply, collected large numbers of swift chargers, strong mules, and splendid palfreys, as well as many fine swords and much armor. As the men of the court appraised it, the Cid accepted it. The Infantes paid the Cid born in a blessed hour the two hundred marks which King Alfonso returned to them, and in addition they borrowed from others, for their own resources were inadequate. Thus, the Infantes emerged from the affair the objects of mockery.

138

The Cid accepted the goods and gave them over into the care of his men. When this demand had been satisfied, they turned to the consideration of another.

"Hear me, my King and lord, I beg of you! I cannot overlook the gravest charge of all. Let every man in this court hear me and share my humiliation. Since the Infantes de Carrión have dishonored me so vilely, I am forced to challenge them.

139

"Tell me, Infantes de Carrión, have I ever done you any wrong, either in jest, or in earnest, or in any other manner? If so, I shall set it right in any manner this court may decide. Why did you tear out the strings of my heart? When you left Valencia, I gave you my daughters, I accorded you the highest honors, and I made you many gifts of great value. If you did not love the girls, you treacherous dogs, why did you take them from Valencia, their inheritance? Why did you beat them with your cinches and rake them with your spurs? Then you deserted them in the Forest of Corpes, exposed to the savage animals and birds of the wild! Because of what you did to them, I charge that you are vile! [14] If you do not give me satisfaction, then let this court pass judgment."

[14] The prelude to the formal issuing of the challenge was *"Menos valedes vos,"* "You are worthless," or "You are worth less [than I]," considered insulting in the highest degree. The expression appears, along with other insults, in the three speeches of challenge issued by the Cid's champions.

The Cid himself does not challenge the Infantes, but leaves it to his vassals, on whose honor the grievance touches.

The challenge to the duel could be made only for reasons of bodily harm (tweaking the beard, slapping the face, etc.) or for offenses involving a man's honor, and not for reasons of material loss. Only those of noble blood could engage in these combats, for in the rigidly stratified society of the Middle Ages the code of honor did not extend to the commoners, and their "honor" could therefore not be affected one way or the other.

140

Then the Count Don García Ordóñez got to his feet. "Hear me, O King, greatest in all Spain! The Cid is an old hand at knowing how to attend these courts that are summoned [by the King]; [15] that is why he has let his beard grow long—to make some men timid and to terrify others.

"The Infantes are of such noble blood that they could not properly consent to take the Cid's daughters even for their concubines, much less for their lawful wives and equals! The Infantes acted entirely within their rights when they deserted them. And so, we have nothing but contempt for what the Cid has said."

"Praise be to God, Lord of heaven and earth!" said the Cid Campeador, as he placed his hand on his beard. "Of course my beard is long, for I have taken good care of it. Why do you try to disparage my beard, O Count? Since this beard first grew, I have ever kept it free of dishonor. No man born of woman has ever laid hand on it, and neither Moor nor Christian has ever plucked a hair of it, as I once did from yours, O Count, in the castle of Cabra. When I captured your castle of Cabra—as well as a tuft of hair from your beard, even the youngsters had a chance to take their pinch from your beard. And my insult to you still stands, for the hair I pulled out has not yet grown back.[16] See, here it is; I have carried it ever since in my purse!"

141

Then the Infante Fernando came to his feet and loudly addressed the assembly. "Enough of your demands, O Cid! We

15 Textual difficulties render uncertain the meaning of this sentence. Menéndez Pidal, whose preference I have followed, lists variant interpretations of the verb (vezós) by five other scholars: "there stands," "behold," "he has prepared himself," etc.

16 A medieval law stipulated a fine for plucking a tuft from a man's beard or pulling out the hair of his head, to be paid in installments until the hair was grown out and the dishonor no longer apparent. This law, however, would not have applied to the Cid.

have repaid you all your money; do not prolong the suit be-
tween us. We belong to the family of the counts of Carrión
and are worthy to wed the daughters of kings or emperors,
not the offspring of some petty nobleman. We were within
our rights in deserting your daughters, and we have brought
no disgrace upon ourselves, but honor instead."

142

The Cid Ruy Díaz fastened his gaze on Pedro Bermúdez.
"Speak up, Pedro the Mute, man of few words! They are my
daughters, but they are your cousins. While these insults are
addressed to me, they fall on your ears, too. If I reply to them,
you will have no chance to answer them in judicial duel."

143

Pedro Bermúdez began to speak; his tongue faltered, and
at first he had trouble with his words; but once he got started
he spoke at great length. "I will tell you, O Cid, your ways
are strange! You always call me Pedro the Mute in court. You
well know that I can do no better at eloquence, but I promise
that I will not be found wanting in action, whatever must be
done.

"Every word you have said, Fernando, is a lie! Your ties
with the Campeador have brought honor to you. I am going
to reveal your true character. Do you remember that day of
the battle near Valencia? You had begged the loyal-hearted
Campeador for the honor of striking the first blows of the
battle. You saw a Moor and started to attack him, but you
turned and fled before he could catch you. If I had not come
to your rescue, that Moor would have made fair game of you.
I rode on past you and engaged the Moor. I was the one who
struck the first blows of the battle, with which I overcame your
foe. I gave you his charger and concealed the truth of the
affair, nor have I ever told a soul about it until this day.
Then you boasted in the presence of the Cid and everybody

else that you had killed the Moor and had become a great hero. Everyone, not knowing what had really happened, believed you. You are very handsome, it is true, but not very much of a man! O you tongue without hands, how is it you are bold enough to speak at all?

144

"Speak up, Fernando, and confess the truth of what I am going to tell next: Do you not recall the time in Valencia that, while the Cid was sleeping, the lion got loose? And tell me, Fernando, what did you do when your terror overcame you? You crawled under the couch of the Cid Campeador! That is exactly what you did, Fernando, and today, therefore, I call you a miserable coward. The rest of us surrounded the couch to protect our lord. When the Cid, the conqueror of Valencia, awoke, he rose from the couch and walked toward the lion, who stood waiting with lowered head and then allowed himself to be taken by the mane and led back into his cage. When the Cid came back to where his vassals were, he asked where his sons-in-law could be, for they were nowhere to be seen.

"I denounce your evil and traitorous person, and I challenge you to the duel. Here in the presence of King Don Alfonso I shall defend against you the honor of the Cid's daughters, Doña Elvira and Doña Sol. I impugn your honor for having cast them away. While they are women and you are men, I say that they are in every way worthier than you. When the joust takes place, by the grace of God, you are going to confess, like the traitor you are, the truth of every charge I have made."

Here ended the words between Pedro Bermúdez and Fernando González.

145

Then Diego González spoke out, "In our veins flows the blood of the most illustrious counts. Would that we had never

entered into these marriages and ties with the family of the
Cid Don Rodrigo! We have never been sorry that we left his
daughters. Let them grieve as long as they live; they will al-
ways be mocked because of what we did to them. This truth
will I uphold in combat against the most valiant foe: We did
ourselves an honor by putting them aside."

146

Then Martín Antolínez got to his feet. "Silence that lying
mouth of yours, you treacherous dog! You, too, can doubtless
remember that affair of the lion. You fled through the door
out into the courtyard, where you hid behind the beam of a
wine press. Never again did you wear that particular mantle
nor that tunic! This will I maintain in combat, nor will any-
thing dissuade me: The daughters of the Cid are in every
respect, because you deserted them, worthier than you. When
the duel is over, you are going to confess yourself a traitor,
false in every word."

147

These two put an end herewith to their charges.

Then Asur González, brother of Diego and Fernando, en-
tered the palace, wearing an ermine mantle and a flowing
tunic; his face was red from the huge meal he had just eaten,
and there was little sense to what he said.

148

"Come now, my lords, was there ever before such nonsense
as this? Whoever would claim that we of the Carrión family
should add to our distinction through this Cid de Vivar? Let
him go back to the river Ubierna to clean the gears of his
mills and collect his pittance of grain for the service he is
accustomed to perform! Who could ever think of uniting such
blood with that of the Carrión family?"

Then Muño Gustioz got to his feet to reply. "Silence, you perfidious, evil traitor! You, who fill your belly before you go to mass and then belch in the face of those you kiss in greeting! You, who have never spoken a word of truth to your equal or to your lord! False to everyone, and above all to your God! I want no part of your sort of friendship. And in combat I will force you to confess that you are all I have called you."

"Enough of these charges," broke in King Alfonso. "God help me, only those who have already challenged are to engage in combat."

Just as they finished speaking, two knights entered the hall; one of them, Ojarra by name, was the petitioner of the Prince of Navarre, and the other, Íñigo Jiménez, the Prince of Aragón's emissary. They kissed King Alfonso's hands and asked for the Cid's daughters in marriage, to be the future queens of Navarre and Aragón, the lawful and honored wives of the princes of those lands. At this the entire court fell silent and attentive.

The Cid Campeador arose. "O King Alfonso, my lord! I thank God for this proposal from Navarre and Aragón. That other time, you, not I, gave my daughters in marriage. And so, their future is in your hands; I shall do nothing without your approval."

The King arose and imposed silence upon the assemblage. "I beg of you, O prudent Cid Campeador, that you approve of this marriage. I shall then give my sanction, and the wedding pact will be affirmed today in this court. From such a match great honor, lands, and fortune will accrue to you."

Rising and kissing the King's hands, the Cid declared, "Since the marriage meets with your approval, my lord, I give my consent."

"May God reward you well," said the King. "To you, Ojarra, and to you, Íñigo Jiménez, I hereby authorize this marriage of the Cid's daughters, Doña Elvira and Doña Sol, to the

Prince of Navarre and the Prince of Aragón. May the Cid give them over as their lawful and honored wives."

The two emissaries rose and kissed the hands of the King, and then of the Cid. The parties exchanged solemn promises to do all or more than the pact required. Nearly everybody in the court was delighted with the proposed union—everybody except the Infantes de Carrión.

Then Minaya Álvar Fáñez rose. "A favor I ask of you, O King and lord! And may it not displease the Cid Campeador that I ask to speak. During all this meeting I have denied none of you that chance, and now I should like to have a word on my own account."

"Gladly, Minaya," said the King. "Say whatever you wish."

"I ask everyone present to hear me, for I have a grave charge to lodge against the Infantes de Carrión. I gave them my cousins in the name of King Alfonso, and they accepted them as their rightful and honored wives. The Cid gave them vast wealth, and yet, to our sorrow, they put his daughters away. I therefore challenge them as foul traitors. You, Infantes, are of the Beni-Gómez family, which has produced counts of worth and valor, but it is clear to us all to what depths the family has fallen these days. I thank God that the Infantes de Navarre and Aragón have asked for the hands of my cousins Doña Elvira and Doña Sol. Once they were your rightful wives in equal station with you, but now you shall kiss their hands and call them 'my lady,' and you shall humbly acknowledge yourselves their servants, no matter how great your distaste. Thanks be to God on high and to King Don Alfonso, the Cid's honor increases. You, Infantes, are everything I have called you! And if anyone wishes to answer or deny my charge, let him know that I am Álvar Fáñez, bold as the boldest!"

Gómez Peláez rose now and said, "To what avail have you spoken thus, Minaya? There are many knights in this court who dare to take up your challenge, and whover disagrees with me will meet his certain downfall. If God grants us his favor in this suit, we shall then know the true worth of your words."

"An end to your quarrels," said the King; "let there be no further challenges. Tomorrow at sunrise the combats between the three pairs who challenged in court will take place."

But the Infantes de Carrión objected. "Give us more time," they pleaded. "It is impossible for us to fight here tomorrow; we shall have to go to the land of Carrión for the duels, for we have given all our arms and war horses to the Campeador."

Turning to the Cid, the King told him to decide where the duels would be held. The Cid answered that he was unwilling to go to Carrión and preferred to return to his Valencia.

"Very well," agreed the King. "Leave your champions and their equipment with me, and I promise, as becomes the duty of lord toward vassal, to be responsible for their welfare and safety; no man, neither count nor any other nobleman, will do them violence.

"In this court I hereby decree that the combats are to take place three weeks from this date, in my presence, on the plains of Carrión. If any should fail to appear, his cause will be lost, and he will be declared vanquished and labeled a traitor."

The Infantes had to accept the King's decision.

The Cid kissed the King's hands. "In your care I leave these three knights of mine; I entrust their safety to you, my lord and master. They are well prepared to do their duty in full. Send them back to me in Valencia, please God, with honors won."

And the King replied, "So be the will of God!"

Then the Cid removed his finely woven cap, bright as the sun, and untied the cord which bound up his beard,[17] presenting a wondrous sight to the eyes of all present. Going up to the Counts Don Enrique and Don Remond, he embraced them and urged them with all his heart to choose whatever they pleased as their gift from him. The same offer was made to others who had favored his cause; some accepted and others

---

[17] Now that financial reparation and arrangements for the judicial combat have been made, the Cid may safely undo his beard and uncover his head.

did not. The Cid declined repayment of the two hundred marks due him from the King; furthermore, the King picked out for himself every gift which caught his fancy.

"A favor I ask of you, O King, for the love of the Creator! Since our affairs are settled, I beg to kiss your hands in farewell and be permitted to set out for Valencia, won by me with great labor."

[Then [18] the Cid ordered that animals and every other necessity of travel be furnished the emissaries of the Princes of Navarre and Aragón, and he sent them on their way.

The King Don Alfonso and all the nobles of his court mounted their horses to ride out of the city with the Cid. When they came to Zocodover, the King said to the Cid, who was riding Babieca, "Don Rodrigo, my vassal, I want you to race that horse of yours, of which I have heard such fine reports."

The Cid began to smile and said, "My lord, there are many noblemen in your following who are capable of doing your bidding in this matter; have them put their horses through their paces."

The King was pleased with the answer, but he insisted, nevertheless, that the Cid race his horse for him.

150

The Cid then touched spurs to the charger, whose blazing speed amazed everybody who was watching.]

"I swear by Saint Isidore of León," exclaimed the King as he made the sign of the cross, "that there is no better man than he in all our realm."

The Cid rode up to his lord Alfonso and kissed his hand. "At your command I raced the swift Babieca, who has no equal in any land, neither Moor nor Christian. Take him; he is yours."

But the King refused the gift. "If I should take him from you," he declared, "the horse would not have so good a rider.

[18] See footnote, p. 3.

A horse like this one fully deserves such a master as you, to conquer Moors in battle and to pursue them. God's curse on anyone who tries to separate the two of you, for you and your steed have brought honor to our throne."

At this, the Cid and the King exchanged the usual formalities of parting, and the royal retinue turned back.

The Campeador was giving his final instructions to those who were to represent him in the combat. "And now, Martín Antolínez, and you, Pedro Bermúdez, and my excellent vassal Muño Gustioz: Fight with the steadfast valor expected of men like you, and see that a satisfactory account of you is brought to me in Valencia."

"There is no need for advice of that sort, my lord," replied Martín Antolínez; "we have accepted this obligation, and it is our duty to fulfill it. You may hear that we have been slain, but vanquished, never."

These words brought pleasure to the one born in a blessed hour, and he bid his friends farewell. The Cid then set out for Valencia, and the King left for Carrión.

Three weeks have passed, and the day of the judicial bouts is at hand. The Cid's champions, under the protection of Alfonso de León, have arrived at the appointed time, anxious to fulfill the obligations entrusted them by their lord. They wait there two days for the Infantes de Carrión, who appear with full equipment of war horses and arms. With their kinsmen, they have formed a plan to catch the Campeador's men unprotected, if they can, in order to kill them, thus bringing dishonor to their lord the Cid. But they make no attempt to carry out their evil plot, so great is their fear of reprisal on the part of Alfonso, the Leonese.

The night before the combat is spent keeping vigil over their arms and praying to God. At length the night passes and dawn is beginning to break. Many illustrious noblemen have gathered at the site, eager to watch the battles; in addition to these, of course, King Don Alfonso is on hand, ready to see that justice shall prevail and that no wrong be committed.

Now, the Cid's men don their armor, the three of them making their plans together as the champions of the same lord.

Elsewhere, the Infantes de Carrión are also arming themselves, as the Count García Ordóñez offers them counsel. They petition King Alfonso to bar the swords Colada and Tizón from the combat so that the Cid's men will not be allowed to fight with them. The Infantes are extremely sorry now that they gave them back. But the King denies their request. "When the arrangements were being made at the court, you did not mention the exclusion of any sword. If your own swords are good, they will serve you well, just as will the swords wielded by the Campeador's men. Away, then, and enter the lists, Infantes de Carrión! You will need to fight with true manliness, for in nothing will the Cid's champions be found wanting. If you leave the field victorious, you will have won great honor for yourselves; and if you are vanquished, do not blame us, for everyone knows that you have brought it all on yourselves."

Now, indeed, do the Infantes de Carrión regret the things they have done; at this point they would give all the wealth in Carrión not to have done them.

The King goes to inspect the Cid's men, who are now fully armed. "We beg you, as our master and King, to be the arbiter of this joust between us and the Carrión faction. Help us to gain justice and ward off foul play. For the Infantes have great numbers of their kinsmen with them, and they may be planning some treachery. Our lord the Cid has placed us in your hands. For the love of God, see that our rights are protected."

"With all my heart will I do so," agrees the King.

Fine, fast war horses are led out to the Cid's knights, who make the sign of the cross over the saddle and promptly mount. Their shields, with heavy bosses in the center, hang from their shoulders, and in their hands they carry their sharp-pointed lances, each flying a pennant. Surrounded by a throng of noblemen, the three knights of the Cid ride out to the plain where the lists have been marked off, each with the same determination to attack his respective foe with all his might.

From the other side of the field come the Infantes de Carrión and a very large band of partisans, for their relatives are quite numerous.

The King appoints judges, who are to pronounce none but a just decree in the case and put an end to any dispute that may arise.

There in the field King Don Alfonso addresses them: "Hear my words, Infantes de Carrión! This combat could have been held in Toledo, but you wished it otherwise. And so I have brought these three knights of the Cid Campeador here to Carrión under my personal guarantee of safety. Now defend your cause, but beware of any perfidious act, for I will thwart with all my might whoever makes such an attempt, and nowhere in all my kingdom shall he find peace."

At these words the Infantes de Carrión are even more disturbed than before.

The judges and the King set up the boundary markers, and the area is cleared. The six combatants are informed that anyone who goes outside the boundaries of the field will be declared vanquished. The spectators draw back on all sides and are instructed to stay six spear lengths away from the boundaries. The knights draw lots for positions and are so placed that no one has to face the sun. The judges leave the field, and the six knights take up positions facing each other.

Thereupon, the Cid's champions advance upon the Carrións, and the Carrións against the Cid's champions, each with his complete attention fixed on his opponent. They hold their shields in front of their bodies and lower their pennant-flying lances; leaning low over the pommels of the saddles, they strike spurs to the horses, and the earth trembles under their swift charge. Not one takes his eyes off his opponent. Three on a side, they meet head on. To the onlookers it appears that they will all be knocked to the ground and killed.

Pedro Bermúdez, who issued the first challenge, clashes with

Fernando González. With complete lack of fear, each aims a blow against the other's shield. The lance of Fernando González passes through Don Pedro's shield, but it misses the target of flesh it has aimed for, and the shaft breaks in two places. Pedro Bermúdez does not fall to earth but holds firm in the saddle and in return for the blow he takes, he strikes one of his own which smashes the center boss of his foe's shield and sends it flying; his lance pierces the shield and strikes the man in the chest near the heart. But the effect of the blow is lessened by the fact that Fernando is wearing a three-fold coat of mail; the two outer layers give way, while the third holds. But this inner layer of mail, along with the shirt and tunic, is driven into the flesh to the depth of a man's hand. Blood begins to spout from his mouth. Fernando's saddle girths snap, not one of them holds fast, and the knight is hurled over the rear of his steed to the ground. Everyone believes he has received his death wound. Pedro Bermúdez, without removing the lance from his adversary's wound, draws his sword, which, as soon as he sees it, Fernando González recognizes as Tizón. "I am vanquished!" he cries out, before the blow can fall. The judges pronounce his defeat, and Pedro Bermúdez leaves him.

151

Martín Antolínez and Diego González charge each other so furiously that both lances are shattered. Then Don Martín draws the sword Colada, and light flashes throughout the field from its bright, clear blade. With it, he strikes a blow on the side of Diego's head which knocks off the metal cap of the helmet; it shears the leather thongs and tears away the hood of mail with its face guard, as well as the cloth cap. The sword scrapes away the hair and causes a wound on the head. The upper part of the head's protective armor falls to the ground, while the lower part remains in place.

At this blow of the mighty Colada, Diego González sees

that he may not escape with his life. He reins his horse around
to face his foe. In his hand he holds a sword, but he lacks the
courage to wield it. Martín Antolínez meets him with his
sword ready and again he strikes him, not with the cutting
edge, but with the flat side, and the Infante begins to scream,
"Help me, O God of glory! Save me, O God, from this sword!"
In fear of the weapon he checks his horse and drives him out
of bounds, leaving the field to Don Martín.

Then the King calls to Martín Antolínez, "Come over here
and join me. By your might you have won this contest."

And the judges concur in the King's declaration.

152

With two of the Cid's champions victorious, let us learn
how Muño Gustioz has fared in his duel with Asur González.
First comes the crash of lance against shield. Asur González,
strong and bold, strikes the shield of Muño Gustioz and
pierces it; although his lance penetrates the other's armor, it
fails to inflict a wound. Muño Gustioz in turn shatters his
opponent's shield at the center boss. The victim's coat of mail
gives him no protection, and he is wounded in the side, but
not near the heart. The spearhead, pennant and all, pierces
his body and sticks out a full six feet on the other side. Twist-
ing the shaft to one side, Muño Gustioz throws the other off
balance in the saddle. When he withdraws the lance, his foe
is toppled to the ground. Shaft, point, and pennant emerge
blood red from the wound. The onlookers are sure that Asur
González is mortally wounded. Muño Gustioz remains poised
over his fallen adversary, ready to strike again with his lance.
But Gonzalo Ansúrez [19] cries out, "Do not strike him, for the
love of God! The end has come; the battle is lost."

Hearing this admission of defeat, the judges decree that the
Carrión faction has lost the suit.

The good King Don Alfonso orders an end to all activity

[19] The historical father of the Infantes, as Menéndez Pidal believes.

on the field; he keeps the arms of the vanquished left on the field.[20] The champions of the noble Campeador withdraw covered with glory, having won the fray, by the grace of God. On the other hand, grave sorrow weighs upon the land of Carrión.

As a precaution against their being attacked, the King starts the Cid's men on their way during the night. Guardedly they travel day and night until they reach Valencia and appear in the presence of the Cid Campeador. They have proven the Infantes de Carrión to be dishonorable; they have accomplished the task assigned them by their lord. Great is the joy of the Cid Campeador! And great is the humiliation of the Infantes de Carrión!

May every knave who insults and then deserts a worthy woman suffer such a fate or even worse!

And so, the dealings with the Infantes de Carrión come to an end—an end sad indeed to them. As for the one born in a blessed hour, all Valencia shares his joy at the honor won by his champions. Stroking his beard, the Cid Ruy Díaz exclaims, "Praise be to the Lord of heaven! The only part of the Carrión estates my daughters came to possess was the affront done to them. Now that they are avenged, they are well rid of those estates. And now I shall give them in marriage again without the slightest taint of shame, no matter who may object."

The Princes of Navarre and Aragón press their suit; arrangements are made at an interview with King Alfonso of León, and the marriages of Doña Elvira and Doña Sol are solemnized. The grandeur of these matches surpasses that of the first, for the father marries his daughters into a loftier station than before. Thus, further honor accrues to the Cid, for his daughters are queens of Navarre and of Aragón. In a later day his descendants will be among the monarchs of Spain, and on all of them will be reflected the glory of the man who was born in a goodly hour.

[20] The king had the right to take the horses, armor, and weapons of those who were vanquished (thereby proven to be traitors) in these judicial jousts.

The Cid, lord of Valencia, passed from this life during the feast of Pentecost—may Christ have mercy on his soul! [21]

These, then, are the deeds of the Cid Campeador; here his story comes to an end.

[21] The Cid of history died in 1099. After his death his widow Doña Jimena remained in Valencia, but was hard pressed to hold it from capture by the Almoravides, the North African tribe which dominated Arabic Spain from 1093 to 1148. Finally in May of the year 1102, Alfonso VI led a relief force to Valencia and removed the defenders of the city to Toledo. From there Doña Jimena returned to Burgos, taking with her the body of the Cid, which was interred in the monastery of San Pedro de Cardeña, later removed to the town hall of Burgos.

BIOGRAPHICAL INDEX [1]

[1] The names of Biblical characters, saints and divinities, and several other proper names to which the poet merely alludes and which have no structural relevance to the epic have been omitted. Most of the notes which follow are to be credited to the work of Ramón Menéndez Pidal.

BERMÚDEZ, PEDRO. Vassal and nephew of the Cid. His historicity is not clearly established. 26, 28-29, 55-56, 65-69 *passim*, 71, 77, 84, 98-99, 105, 109, 113-14, 120, 122-23

BIRBÓN, COUNT DON. He attends the court of Toledo; however, his historicity seems doubtful. 103

BÚCAR. One of the Moorish kings of Morocco. The name Búcar is linked with that of a famous Almorávide general, Sir ben Abu-Beker; he, however, outlived the Cid. 82-83, 86-89 *passim*

CID CAMPEADOR, THE. DÍAZ DE VIVAR, RUY [RODRIGO]. Vassal of King Alfonso VI and the hero of the epic. He won his title of Campeador, the champion, from the Arabs, through successful single combat with the enemy's champion during the war between Sancho of Navarre and Sancho of Castile. He is also called the lord, or conqueror, of Valencia, and to him are applied the epithets the battler, the leader, the exile, the knight, the one born in a blessed hour, the one who girt the sword in a favored hour, and epithets referring to his beard.

DÍAZ, ÁLVAR. He is lord of Oca, the King's enemy in Alfonso's court. A figure in the courts of Sancho II, Alfonso VI, and Doña Urraca until his death in 1111, he was the brother-in-law of Count García Ordóñez. 72, 103

ELVIRA, DOÑA. She is one of the Cid's two daughters. It is a historical fact that the Cid and Jimena had two daughters named Cristina and María. "Sol" and "Elvira" may have been familiar names more commonly applied to them. As related in the epic, Cristina (Elvira) married an Infante of Navarre named Ramiro, the grandson of García, King of Navarre; their son, García Ramírez, became King of Navarre, and their granddaughter married King Sancho III of Castile. María (Sol) was married to Count Ramón Berenguer III of Barcelona, not to an Infante de Aragón. 13-15 *passim*, 30, 32, 49, 52, 54-55, 58-59, 61, 64, 68-69, 71, 73-74, 77-78, 89, 91-100 *passim*, 104, 109, 114, 116-17, 125

ENRIQUE, COUNT DON. Count of Porto and one of the magistrates of the court of Toledo. He was the fourth son of Henry of Burgundy, great-grandson of King Robert II of France, the cousin of the Count Don Remond, the nephew of King Alfonso's wife Constanza, and the husband of Alfonso's daughter Teresa. Count Enrique died in 1114 in the campaigns waged by Queen Urraca (Remond's widow) against Alfonso, the the Battler of Aragón. 103, 104, 106-7, 118

FÁÑEZ, ÁLVAR. The Cid's nephew and "right arm." Actually, Álvar Fáñez was not so constant a companion of the Cid as he was in the epic. If he did indeed accompany the Cid into exile, it was for only a short time, for documents show that he was elsewhere most of the time while the Cid was in exile. The epithet "Minaya" used in connection with his name may have the etymological meaning of "brother," signifying the close feeling of the Cid for this relative who was not only his chief counselor, but upon whom he relied to perform the most important missions. 5-6, 13, 18, 20-23 *passim*, 25-26, 30-37 *passim*, 44, 48-58 *passim*, 62-64 *passim*, 66-69 *passim*, 71, 75-76, 78-79, 84, 87, 89-90, 92, 98-99, 104-5, 117

FÁRIZ. Moorish emir sent by King Tamín to besiege the Cid at Alcocer. He is probably a fictitious character. 31, 33

FROILA, COUNT DON. He attends the court of Toledo. He appears frequently in documents of the period as the Count of León, of Aguilar, of Astorga, and as the Count Don Remond's major-domo. Count Don Froila was Doña Jimena's brother. 103

GALVE. Moorish emir sent by King Tamín to besiege the Cid at Alcocer. He is probably a fictitious character. 31

GARCÍA, GALINDO. Vassal of the Cid, a knight from Aragón. He is not known to history. 20, 30, 71, 105

GONZÁLEZ, ASUR. Probably the older brother of Diego and Fernando González, the Infantes de Carrión. The genealogy of the Beni-Gómez family has been established by Me-

néndez Pidal, but there seems to be some small doubt that the characters of the epic correspond entirely to the persons of history. 52, 77, 103, 115, 124

GONZÁLEZ, DIEGO. One of the Infantes de Carrión. Menéndez Pidal, despite contrary evidence offered by other scholars, believes in the historical authenticity of Diego and Fernando González. 52-53, 66, 68-70 *passim*, 72-79 *passim*, 81-84 *passim*, 87-98 *passim*, 100-103 *passim*, 106-15 *passim*, 117-18, 120-25 *passim*

GONZÁLEZ, FERNANDO. One of the Infantes de Carrión (see Diego González). 52-53, 66, 68-70 *passim*, 72-79 *passim*, 81-84 *passim*, 87-98 *passim*, 100-103 *passim*, 106-15 *passim*, 117-18, 120-23 *passim*, 125

GUSTIOZ, MUÑO. Vassal of the Cid. After the death of the Cid, the historical Muño Gustioz remained in the company of Doña Jimena, as is attested to in a document of 1113. 55-56, 71, 77, 83, 100-102 *passim*, 105, 116, 120, 124

JERÓNIMO, BISHOP DON. The cleric whom the Cid appoints Bishop of Valencia. The historical facts of this bishop's life coincide essentially with the part he played in the epic. He remained in Valencia after the Cid's death, was sent to Castile for help against the besieging Almorávides, and left Valencia with Doña Jimena and the other defenders of the city in May, 1102. He was Bishop of Salamanca and Zamora until

mez Díaz, Count of Saldaña and Carrión, he died in 1101. He took part in the signing of a document with Álvar Díaz and Diego González, also members of the Carrión faction mentioned in the epic. 117

PÉREZ, DIEGO. He is one of the noblemen defeated and captured by the Cid in the battle against the King of Granada at the beginning of the epic. 3

RAQUEL AND VIDAS. The moneylenders of Burgos who are deceived by the chests filled with sand. The incident in which they were involved probably belongs to folklore. 8-13 *passim*, 54

REMOND, COUNT DON. Count of Galicia, the principal magistrate of the court of Toledo. He was a man of even more importance in the court of King Alfonso VI than his cousin Count Enrique, perhaps because the latter was married to a natural daughter of the King, while Count Don Remond was married to Alfonso's legitimate daughter. He extended his domain to include all of Portugal, but was in turn dispossessed of part of it by his cousin Count Enrique. Alfonso promised to make his son-in-law Remond heir to the thrones of Léon and Castile, but the Count died in 1107, two years before the King. His son became the Emperor Alfonso VII. 103-4, 106-7, 109-10, 118

SALVADÓREZ, ÁLVAR. Vassal of the Cid. He appears inconspicu-

ously in documents of the time of the reign of Alfonso VI, perhaps because he followed the Cid into exile. 20, 30, 62, 71, 105

SÁNCHEZ, FORTÚN. Son-in-law of the King of Navarre, he is one of the noblemen defeated and captured by the Cid in the battle against the King of Granada at the beginning of the epic. 3

SÁNCHEZ, LOPE. He is a bother of Fortún Sánchez, one of the noblemen defeated and captured by the Cid in the battle against the King of Granada at the beginning of the epic. 3

SANCHO, ABBOT DON. Abbot of the monastery of San Pedro de Cardeña near Burgos, in whose charge the Cid leaves his wife and children when he goes into exile. The Abbot is one of the few fictitious characters in the epic. 14-16 *passim*, 18, 49, 54

SOL, DOÑA. One of the Cid's two daughters (*see* Elvira, Doña). The Doña Sol of the epic was in real life named María Rodríguez, the second daughter of the Cid. She was married to Ramón Berenguer III, Count of Barcelona, not to an Infante de Aragón, as related in *The Cid*. 13-15 *passim*, 30, 32, 49, 52, 54-55, 58-59, 61, 64, 68-69, 71, 73-74, 77-78, 89, 91-100 *passim*, 104, 109, 114, 116-17, 125

TAMÍN. Moorish King of Valencia who sent his generals Fáriz and Galve to besiege the Cid at Alcocer. He is a legendary character. 26-27, 34

TÉLLEZ, DIEGO. Vassal of Álvar

Fáñez, governor of San Este-
ban de Gormaz, he was a his-
torical person and lived at a
time and in a place which
would have permitted him to
take part in the action of the
epic. 98

VIDAS. *See* Raquel.

YÚSUF. Moorish King of Mo-
rocco. Historically, the Moor-
ish emperor himself did not
lead the expedition against Va-
lencia, but sent his nephew,
Mohámed ben Ayixa, who was
defeated by the Cid about 1095
near Valencia. 59-60, 63, 65, 67

6694